EMBRACE THE POWER WITHIN

By

Veronica Lavender

First published 10/04/2014

ISBN-13: 978-1497533714

ISBN-10: 1497533716

Other Books by Author

The Essential Creativity of Awareness

Parallel Lives

The Empowered Affirmations Balancing Technique

Jack The Ripper & The Ghost of Mary Jane Kelly

ACKNOWLEDGEMENTS

I would like to say thank you to my children, Debbie, David and Karen who have given me the love and support whilst pursuing my dreams. They continue to be a great inspiration to me with their encouragement. To my dear friends who have given me hours of discussions and debates on all aspects of spirituality.

I would like to thank all readers of my books and the many clients who have attended the different workshops and meditation classes and the one to one consultations. You have inspired me which has allowed me to gain a greater understanding of how the mind, body and soul works together and influences all that we do. Thank you.

INTRODUCTION

Our soul's vibration holds the secrets of our divinity which allows us to understand, and overcome any negative issues that has affected our lives or well being state. But first, we have to reconnect with the ascended vibration of our soul; within this vibration is our true identification and uniqueness. It holds the collective consciousness of which we have ever been, and we can tap into this collective vibration within any incarnate life. We do this with the intention of obtaining from our blueprint the secrets of our gifts, skills and abilities, the hidden messages, and the memories of our pre-agreed arrangement of our life's purpose, and the infinite knowledge and wisdom from all lifetimes that would set us free within this lifetime.

The details of our past lives are stored within the blueprint of our soul; they form parts of our characteristics, and inherited traits of our individual characters. Every one of us at sometime or other has experienced Déjà vu memories, and the instant feeling of knowing someone that we've just met, being aware of an infinite connection. We have all dreamed of places we've never been too, and had visions within our dreams or waking states of the memories of some forgotten time. We have experienced skills and talents that have come naturally to us, but also our vacations when suddenly we find ourselves doing a job that is second nature to us. The memories held within our soul holds an in-sight into our truth of who we really are, and what we've already accomplished or achieved.

The Age of Aquarius is called The Golden Age, and will approximately last for 2,150 years, and it's the spiritual reawakening of all. Enlightened spirituality is the rising of the collective consciousness to heal a wounded world, and our souls. New beginnings are often disguised as painful endings as we lift the veils of our painful deceptions of our illusions, and ignorance of our higher conscious self. It is important that we embrace change within our lives, all being a natural part of our continued growth and survival in a world where there is so much unrest.

We must focus on the energy of our higher consciousness in order to let go of the old ways of doing and perceiving, and allow us to embrace a better future. We do this by participating in this golden age of limitless potential. Once we realise that we no longer need to fight for survival, instead we must embrace this new beginning, where we can evoke a new world.

The Age of Aquarius is the beginning of a new way of life, with us all participating in the transformational period. We will all go through a series of initiations, before we can really appreciate what's happening to us within this new cyclic age. At present we are over populated with lots of souls walking our earth plane, whether physically or spiritually, and this is because all souls are taking part in the transformation of this evolutionary age of our soul's quest, with the continuance of a journey into unknown territory. We will all at sometime or other in the future evolve to other dimensions within the solar system of our universe. So let's put our best foot forwards has our futures positively await us!

Thousands of people are quietly awakening to their higher consciousness, and thousands more have already been awakened. Although people may derive inspiration, moral codes, and even wisdom from the religious texts or great authors of spiritual matters, it's all a second hand experience. When we've awakened to our enlightened-self we'll experience inspiration and wisdom first hand, and our own moral codes is intuitive and pure, because we can do no more than to act with integrity in all that we do.

This is a new beginning for us all, and we must not give into the uncertainty of what our future holds, but to be living it in the Now would allow us the opportunity to explore the next evolutionary age with confidence. We will experience some incredible in-sights into our higher conscious abilities, and of the natural gifts of extraordinary phenomenon. With some of us having out of body experiences, astral travel, remote vision, and the third eye opening which alters our state of awareness. This allows us to be more accepting of these unique and instinctive gifts of survival, helping us to maintain balance and harmony within all things.

There is nothing to fear within our gifts, skills or abilities, for they are our natural attributes of the higher consciousness that allows these gifts to be activated, so we can achieve great things for us, but naturally. We are pure energy being affected by the changing energy of our planet, and we are all participating in the purification and cleansing of not just our planet but us also, and with the restoration of balance and harmony within all aspects of our lives, helping us all to achieve world peace.

When we have become enlightened we can face our future with confidence and conviction, and our futures hold huge potential as we become the person that we use to be, but centuries ago. Once we have become our higher conscious self, and successfully accessed all that we need, we will be living our lives in truth with us manifesting all that we desire naturally and effortlessly.

Enlightenment means to be enlightened to our true self, the truth, and our ability to predict the future for us. We can't predict what might happen in the future as we have no control over the different situations, but we can predict what we want to happen for us. We must have pure intention and conviction when projecting what we want to achieve or accomplish but in an enlightened state. We would then be naturally accepting of all situations, with us waiting patiently for them to materialize.

Embracing the power within is to embrace our high conscious self in its truest form. Over many lifetimes and even throughout this lifetime, we will at sometime or other have disconnected from our higher conscious self. The disconnection of our higher conscious self happens because we've stopped believing in us or we don't trust or have faith in us anymore. There are numerous reasons as to why this disconnection happens; but it leaves us struggling within our everyday lives, with us having to work harder to achieve our dreams or goals. We should be all doing less within our lives in order to achieve more, and not doing more to achieve less, as we all seem to do at sometime or other!

After every incarnate life our soul returns back to the source where it reconnects to the blueprint of its origin. The purpose of returning to the source after death is to understand any trauma, anguish, emotional imbalance, illness or disease that's happened to us whilst on the earth plane. It is important for us to understand what our lives had been all about, and to what was expected from us. The truth of the different situations is realised, with us gaining the deeper understanding of our agreement that we pre-made before coming into our present life. We need this information in order to fulfil our life's purpose, and then learn from all experiences.

Did we successfully recall our pre-agreed arrangement or those hidden memories of long ago with the intention of reinstating our higher consciousness, and ascended self or did we fail? If so, we'll need to come back again to another life at some other time, and start the learning process all over again.

When we achieve our life's purpose, and gain the understanding of our lessons, we'll overcome them. This gives us the infinite knowledge and wisdom that helps to reinstate the ultimate connection of the existence of our ascended self, and enables us to finally EMBRACE THE POWER WITHIN!

PREFACE

Our soul's journey and quest is about us integrating with every positive aspect of us, and that includes our past incarnate lives that are relevant to our ascension. We have all been on our soul's journey over the centuries, gathering the infinite knowledge and wisdom that would allow us to become our collective consciousness once again.

We can't prepare for the unknown, we can only prepare ourselves for what we want to be or do. Spirituality has come a full circle because in the past we needed these learning's or teachings in order to open us up to the higher vibrations of our enlightened self. We are now in an Age of Aquarius where these changes are spontaneous, with us all going through the evolutionary age of the activation of our higher consciousness. Our higher conscious vibration is the evolutionary energy of the Kundalini which promotes the spiritual awakening of humankind.

We are all on our personal pathways to enlightenment, and it's a journey that's spanned over many lifetimes with us all getting close to achieving our soul's quest. We do not have to be on a religious path or even a spiritual path in order to attain being enlightened, as it's a natural process of life of being open to the truth of all things. We experience life with us not always being our truth, but as we seek the understanding of any given situation or circumstance that we find ourselves in, we will eventually recognise the different levels of truth as we evolve and learn.

Over the years of being self-aware and gaining the understanding of what had happened to me, I was able to understand that by being totally honest with myself I could expose the truth of what was happening, and the reasons as to why? Everything that we do is influenced by our perception of what we think has happened because of our emotional or mental states, and also the influence of our life's purpose. We get confused at times, because everything we do is about seeking the truth, but our levels of truth alters with our state of consciousness. We must see, hear and speak our truth at all times and with clarity, and from that moment on we access our truth instantly.

Prosperity awaits us all but first it's about the cleansing and purification of our sub-conscious and conscious minds, which will set us free from our limiting belief's in order to embrace a world of great phenomena. The journey of self-discovery is a journey of the self back to the self; it's about reinventing and rediscovering our authentic self once more, allowing us to empower our true-self, and transforming our life, and all lives consciously. This is the evolutionary journey of the soul's quest, and it's potentially an exciting journey of self discovery!

Our hidden agendas have us travelling many pathways in life and sometimes blindly, with our emotions get the better of us out of desperation or frustration. We then make others or even the different situations within our lives a projection of our insecurities, and we focus on them because it distracts us from ourselves, with us not sorting our own issues out. We all owe it to us to take responsibility for us, and release our negative beliefs or imbalances in order to embrace our unique power within, and our higher consciousness.

Our past lives give us an in-sight into our true-selves, revealing hidden messages and the secrets to our present lifetime. These important in-sights allow us to gain the valuable information that would allow us to fully understand what our lives are all about. This information helps us to evolve with the continuance of the soul's quest, and to become whole and complete once more.

The information about our past lives helps us to reinstate equilibrium within our everyday lives, allowing us to realign to the positive attributes of our past lives that unleashes our limitless potential. Because within every past life that we address the more in-sight into our true-selves, and that of our characters. Then we're able to draw from those lives the positive attributes of us which are our unrealised potential.

My life would have been a lot easier if I'd known what my hidden agenda or life's purpose was all about, it would have made me more accepting of the experiences I'd had, good or bad. Hindsight is a wonderful thing but now I know what my life's learning's were about, I can go on to teach others who want to learn theirs sooner rather than later, because then we'd all save us from a lot of pain or grief, and more importantly time. We have to re-educate us to give ourselves more time to enjoy what we do have within our lives, but to enjoy whole heartily, healthy, joyfully and wisely. This is the life that our creator intended for us all, but only after completing the first part of our soul's quest in order to overcome our life's purpose, and continue the journey of the soul by achieving ascension.

At times I personally struggled with my life, with me just going through the motions of my daily chores, and I justified why I wasn't achieving by working hard for others to succeed because I didn't believe in me anymore. I seemed to live my life in the shadow of my former self, always looking back to some idyllic time when I felt my life was happier. I wanted my old life back at times, the life I'd had before I was divorced, but I was in denial of my feelings or should I say, I wouldn't allow myself to acknowledge my true feelings so I kept them suppressed for years which caused me great pain and grief.

The realisation that I'd also had very little self-belief, faith or trust in me became evident, and I wasn't even sure that I'd ever really loved myself at all, only to discover this was what my life's purpose had been all about. I'd been searching for a love that only I could give myself, and it was a journey that had started years earlier with my grandmother, who didn't seem to like or even love me. Over the years I tried my best to get her to love me, and I now realised I'd been doing the same ever since not just with my grandmother but all who came into my life. I did this by giving too much of myself to others thinking it would buy me their love, only it didn't.

Life is about us overcoming our life's purpose in order to reconnect with our higher conscious self and truth. This process sets us free from the restraints and restrictions that we'd held ourselves too, giving us conviction and courage in all that we do which allows us to be living our lives to the full.

We do not find ourselves within the different spiritual pathways but through them, where we can reignite the embers of our ascended self, and embrace the uniqueness of us and our limitless potential by allowing us to be the best we can be, and to live our lives truthfully and consciously.

CONTENTS

CHAPTER 1

THE SOUL'S JOURNEY

At the beginning of creation beings originated from a soul or essence that was created by God. These souls then divided into two, forming one male and one female soul, in order to co-create gathering human experiences over many incarnate lives. These souls are referred to as twin flames, and within our soul is the blueprint of all lifetimes and beyond, and holds the records of all that we've accomplished since time began, and too whom we have ever been, including our origin.

Our soul has travelled through many lifetimes experiencing different incarnate lives, with some of us having evolved from other planets. The soul is our higher conscious self, and stored within its vibration are the secrets that allow us to unlock our sub-conscious minds once more. We can then activate our hidden gifts, skills and abilities of our higher consciousness, which allows us to evolve effortlessly through any lifetime in order to be ascended once more.

When we become our higher conscious self, and have understood and overcome our life's purpose, we then pay back our karmic debt for all that we'd got wrong or done wrongly over the many incarnate lives that we've had. When this is done we gain the infinite knowledge and wisdom, derived from understanding our life's purpose and experiences, allowing us to actively seek, and achieve an enlightened status that allows our consciousness to grow. The intention is for us to evolve towards ascension, a spiritual level of existence that allows us to become all knowing once again!

On completion of this evolutionary journey is the transition of our soul's quest, and allows twin flames to reunite in order to ascend or return back to the soul's original origin. Each individual will take their journey of ascension when they

1

have successfully completed their life's journey as we know it, and have totally understood the soul's existence on the earth plane. We all evolve at different times, and through the dimensional levels of all existence with one main purpose, and that's to reach ascension whilst still here on the earth plane, as this is something we haven't done in a very long time.

Twin flame souls were the crusaders through history, fighting for truth, honour, freedom and justice. During other lifetimes they would meet other souls that they were compatible with, these souls were classed as soul-mates. Within these lives they would share life's experiences with them in order to learn from, with us at times experiencing different relationships such as brother, sister, husband, wife, and so on. These soul-mate relationships got stronger through the different incarnate lifetimes that they'd shared together, whilst experiencing all the different aspects of life. This gave us the opportunity to understand how our lives should be lived by us becoming more accepting of all experiences in order to learn the truth within each aspect of our lives.

Meeting our soul-mates was part of our life's purpose in order to for us to evolve successfully, because within our sub-conscious we hold the memories of the happy and contented times that we'd spent together. Then we had other lifetimes where we would meet our twin flame with the intention of reliving the memories of blissful times that we shared together, which made us feel whole and complete.

Twin flame relationships experienced incredible powers that reignited whenever they were back together, for each holds what's missing from within the other. When these twin souls depart their final earthly life they returned back to the source, reuniting as a twin flame connection, which allows them to integrate back to their original origin in preparation for the next stage of evolution. These twin flames then become ascended, maybe living another lifetime on a different planet or residing on another level of existence here on the earth plane?

2

Our mission in life is to reconnect with the vibration of our soul which allows us to understand our life's purpose, and overcome our life's lessons, good or bad. This process will allow us to heal our lives with the infinite knowledge, and wisdom that's stored within the collective vibration of our personal and spiritual truth held within our blueprint.

When we become our truth, we can then achieve our limitless potential, with our higher conscious self evolving by seeking enlightenment. The journey of enlightenment enables us to reconnect with our ascended self once more, whilst we're still here on the earth plane, strengthening our relationship with all things, the creator, and universal energy that sustains all life.

Our life's purpose is because we've disconnected from our higher conscious self, a process created from non acceptance of things that's happen to us, and we may have disconnected centuries ago. The soul's purpose is to evolve beyond the limitations and restriction that we hold ourselves too because of our perception of life's trials and tribulations. The way we perceive our life's experiences denotes in how we then allow the negative undertones to affect us, which then creates emotional imbalances within, affecting our mind, body or soul, in some way.

We have all experienced every imaginable life over the centuries, with some lives being very positive, and other lives being hard work. We often struggle with our everyday lives, with some of us making the same mistakes over and over again, which leaves us confused about life! Within any lifetime we'll have experienced positive and joyous times, with negative issues being a natural process of life as we try to solve our problems, easily and effortlessly. At times, we do not always achieve what we set out to achieve, leaving us feeling a failure or doubting us and our abilities.

Our soul's vibration holds the secrets of our divinity which allows us to understand, and overcome any negative issues that have affected our lives or well being state. But first, we have to reconnect with the ascended vibration of our soul; within this vibration is our true identification and uniqueness. It holds the collective consciousness of which we have ever been, and when we tap into this collective vibration within any incarnate life, it's to obtain the secrets, and the infinite wisdom that would set us free.

Our individual consciousness of any lifetime changes depending on what we've learnt or overcome. So depending on our pre-agreed level of consciousness that's set at the time of our birth; for example say we have a vibration set at two hundred on the scale of conscious awareness for this lifetime, but we had attained five hundred in another lifetime, this lifetime would be about raising our vibration from two hundred to five hundred, by overcoming our pre-agreed life's purpose or lessons, with the reactivation of our higher consciousness.

Once we had achieved the higher vibration, it allows our soul to naturally continue its evolutionary journey to evolve beyond our limitations. We then achieve ascension with a vibrational level of seven hundred plus on the scale of conscious awareness, with the highest level being thousand which is the vibration that Jesus Christ vibrated at. His vibration allowed others to heal their lives as long as they were open to the higher energies but also he spoke the infinite knowledge and wisdom that they all needed to hear to reignite within them the truth of their higher conscious selves once more.

The details of our past lives are stored within the blueprint of our soul; they form parts of our characteristics, and inherited traits of our individual characters. Every one of us at sometime or other has experienced Deja vu memories, and the instant feeling of knowing someone that we've just met, being aware of an infinite connection. We have all dreamed of places we've never been too, and had visions within our dreams or waking states of the memories of some forgotten time. We have experienced skills and talents that have come

4

naturally to us, but also our vacations when suddenly we find ourselves doing a job that is second nature to us. The memories held within our soul holds an in-sight into our truth, who we really are, what we've achieved, whom we've ever been, and too what we have done good or bad. Also stored within our consciousness are the memories of what we pre-agreed too, and the promise we made to persevere and succeed in achieving them.

We need to reconnect with the hidden messages or secrets about our present and past lifetimes that are relevant to us within this life, is in order to maintain power over the decisions that we make. Throughout our lifetime we are given many opportunities to overcome our lessons, with synchronicities and coincidences of life coming into play naturally. This helps us to achieve our goals, and gain deeper understanding to our truth and abilities, allowing us to manifest our dreams naturally by connecting to the oneness within us, this being our power of intention and conviction!

We have all experienced every possible scenario within the different lives that we've had, from being wealthy or poor, happy or sad, healthy or ill, male or female, let alone committing all of the deadly sins such as greed, envy, murder and so on. We also experience the same soul families or groups, all evolving at different times, in different places but coming together from time to time to learn from, and encourage each other onwards.

We also have to pay back our karmic debt or having a karmic debt paid back to us, what goes around, comes around, good or bad! So what we have done to others, we'll have done to us! That's why we must never judge others because we do not honestly know what we've done. I believe we've done it all good or bad, and this lifetime is about a small proportion of the emotional imbalances that we've created for us or others. It takes many lifetimes to complete the journey of the soul's unrest, before we can become enlightened to our truth in order to embrace our unique power within.

Our unique abilities are our gifts, skills and talents that naturally allow us to overcome any problem effortlessly. Our inner wisdom prevails, a knowing or vision of clairvoyance, an inner hearing of clairaudience, or even our intuition or gut reaction of clairsentience. These are our higher conscious skills allowing us to know the in-sights into our deepest thoughts, feelings and about some phenomenon or other.

With the deeper understanding of our life's experiences or lessons, allows us to alter our perception of how we then perceive our lives and to how we allow life's experiences to affect us, consciously or sub-consciously. How we perceive our different problems denotes in how we allow the imbalances to affect us, and to where we store those imbalances within.

We are given many opportunities to overcome our disharmony or imbalances within but at times we refuse to admit there may be a problem. By being self and body aware we can recognised the disharmonious situations and by reconnecting to our unique abilities we can eradicate any imbalance, illness or disease, and restore a well being state, once we have fully understood and overcome our lessons.

When our soul decides to be reborn into another lifetime, the details of our proposed life's purpose and lessons are pre-discussed! We are given in-sight into our talents and abilities, and we make promises in order to overcome our life's purpose, and to achieve our limitless potential. At the moment of our birth the memories of which are stored within the collective vibration of our soul, and we have to wait until the agreed time in order for us to start the journey so we can reconnect with, which allows us to activate the information needed to overcome our purpose effortlessly, and gain the truth about our existence within this lifetime, all being part of the divine plan.

We will have chosen our parents before we came into this lifetime, because their negative traits perfectly match our learning's, and we'll have chosen the different circumstances and situations that will happen to us. The process of the soul's journey takes many lifetimes to complete with us all having started this journey a very long time ago. When this quest is completed, we choose to live the life that was intended for us, which allows us to ascend to the higher dimensional levels of existence having freed our souls, whether within this life or another lifetime!

Within our souls blueprint is stored the genetic learning's from our ancestors, the historic learning's from past lives which allows us to achieve the overall learning's of all things, and helps us to release some of the worlds mass negativity which restores peace and harmony, within all lives eventually. First, we must restore inner peace within us, by the process of purification and cleansing of all aspects of our lives, and this is part of the world's purification and cleansing process, in readiness of embracing The Golden Age that we are now living in and it's the age of great potential and opportunities.

As we continue to travel along life's path our learned behaviours from others, our negative beliefs, traits or programs, and that of our life's purpose or lessons starts to unfold. We begin the process of trying to understand what's expected of us, and too what life's trail's and tribulations are all about. The soul's journey is to overcome the negative imbalances from our pre-agreed past lifetimes as well as this one in order to evolve, and become our truth and higher conscious self once more.

After every incarnate life our soul returns back to the source where it reconnects to the blueprint of its origin. The purpose of returning to the source after death is to understand any trauma, anguish, emotional imbalance, illness or disease that's happened to us whilst on the earth plane. It is important for us to understand what our lives are all about, and to what's expected from us. It's about the truth and us gaining the deeper understanding of our agreement, so did we successfully recall those hidden memories, and reinstate our higher conscious or ascended self or did we fail and need to come back again into another lifetime, and start the learning process all over again.

When we achieve our life's purpose or lessons it will give us the infinite knowledge and wisdom that reinstates the ultimate connection of our existence, and enables us to become our truth. Our truth is the real reasons behind everything we do, and it can't be justified or argued with, and when we're successfully aware of the truth of our actions, our lives become effortless. We then achieve things beyond our wildest dreams by becoming our limitless potential, all because we'd embraced the power within us that sets us free.

CHAPTER 2

LIFE'S PURPOSE

Our life's purpose and journey begins at the moment of our conception where we absorb vibrational influences' from our parents. We then experience life as baby in the womb, and whatever we're exposed to either by our families or the people around them would continue to influence us. From the moment we're born we continue to be influenced by what is needed in order to help us understand and overcome our life's purpose, later on within our lives.

The journey of our soul is about experiencing all aspects of life, with the interaction of our parents, siblings, grandparents, and others that we come into contact with on a day to day basic. We are also influenced by what we see on television, read in books or newspapers, and even the internet but more importantly we respond to the vibrational forces of the universe, the earth, and mankind.

When we're born it's to parents, and their families and friends, who experience an overwhelming sense of unconditional love. In that moment it's about the purity of a new life, and the fact that a miracle as just been performed. People come together to celebrate the safe arrival of a new life, it's about the giving and receiving of unconditional love that has no hidden agenda. Babies display the positive qualities of love, faith, trust, and belief in all around them in order to be protected and care for, whilst they are nurtured.

All parents have great intentions, and a responsibility to their children for the rest of their lives. But at times it can all go wrong as we're left struggling to even comprehend what's happened to us or others, and we're often left to pick up the pieces as we try to overcome what's happened. This is when our life's purpose really starts to unfold, and we set off on our

9

own personal journey of our trying to make sense of our life's lessons or experiences, and too what they are all about. The majority of us have happy childhoods, but there are some who do not, and the most dreadful of situations happen to them, with us all asking the question as to why do these things happen or why do people act so cruelly or are uncaring towards others?

Our life's purpose is to understand what our lessons are all about, and by recognising the synchronicities or coincidences of life, helps us to understand the different experiences because everything within our lives happens for a reason, even though those reasons are not always clear until later on. For example, my grandmother gave me a hard time and was always picking on me, I could not understand why at the time! But later in life, I realised she'd treated me the way she had to make me work harder in every aspect of my life, in order to understand the need of self-love, belief, faith and trust in myself. Unbeknown to me at the time, but part of my life's purpose was to reinstate self-love, belief, faith and trust within me, and my grandmothers actions allowed me to recognise that fact, but not as a child but later in life as an adult.

When people join the army their spirit is broken by the intensive training they have to go through in order to get rid of any negative fears, beliefs, programs etc and then they are rebuilt by empowerment of the self to survive any situation or circumstance. The experience strengthens the mind, body and soul but depending on what they are exposed too, each individual will react differently because of their definition of the qualities of commitment, courage, focus, intention, confidence, strength, and a will to succeed in all they do.

The process of life is very similar to preparing for a life in the army, it's about life's experiences, and character building by what we're exposed too, and how we perceive and deal with each challenge. We all need commitment in what we do, which gives us strength of character and intention to fulfil our dreams or goals, and to overcome life's challenges confidently.

Through my process of growing up, my negative traits were brought into play, I started to experience the disharmony within, and at the time I did not comprehend or was even aware of what it was all about! So I found I would look to others for love or approval, doing the different things to please or to be noticed. The more I did, the more that was expected from me, making me try even harder. I did this because I felt that what I did wasn't good enough, not realising at the time that I was trying to fill a void within. Years later recognising that the void within was a lack of self love?

The lack of self-love had affected every area of my life, with me not loving myself enough in order to put myself first, always doing things for others just to prove my love. I did not realise that the lack of self love for me had left me wanting others to show their love for me, but if you don't love yourself, who can? So when someone asked me years later, how much do you love yourself on a scale of one to ten, ten being you do! My reply was two out of ten, and with the realisation that I also had no self-faith, belief or trust in myself, and I realised that I was experiencing low self esteem and no-worth which robbed me of my confidence.

This was a process derived from looking to others for recognition and acceptance, all brought on because my life's lesson was to understand the importance of self love, faith, belief, and trust. Because without them I'd looked to others for what I felt was missing within my life, not recognising that what I'd been searching for all these years was self-love and it was already within me. All I needed to do was acknowledged and understand the importance of loving myself completely, because if not, we end up falling out of love with life!

Over the years I'd lost touch with the responsibility to myself, no one's fault but my own, I always considered myself to be a good wife, and doting mother. Strange though it may seem, I wasn't even sure when I'd started the process of procrastination, beating myself up at every opportunity or taking advice as criticism, which resulted in me losing my self-worth, confidence and faith in my own abilities. The thing is you never realise this at the time, it only becomes evident later on. I had allowed others to put me down; they became too demanding and inconsiderate, the more I did the more they wanted me to do. Not realising that this too, was about their lack of trust, faith and belief in themselves and their own abilities, the mirror image of me.

What happened to me I had un-consciously allowed to happen, as it was all part of my life's lessons or experiences. So the negative traits of my learning's started to influence my life, I felt unhappy all because I'd not recognised my own imbalances or the disharmony within. I totally dismissed the inner voice of my soul, gently trying to guide me forwards. All brought on by my ignorance to my inner self and truth, and the disconnection from my higher conscious self which had created the unrest that I felt within. I got to the point where I did not recognise myself anymore, what had happened to me had left me in a vulnerable state. Leaving me craving for some idyllic time when I felt happier, not realising that all within my life was as it should be, all being part of the divine plan in order for me to learn from.

My life had changed dramatically, and the journey that followed was all that I had pre-agreed too long ago, because my life experiences and some of the choices I'd made left me really unhappy and struggling with certain aspects within my life. The pain that I'd created for myself was so bad that I wanted out of this lifetime. I'd lost confidence in me and my ability to change certain situations within my life.

The real test in life comes from facing our demon's head on, but at the time I was not aware of the real reasons behind the situation or circumstance that I'd found me to be in. The vital information about my life's purpose was not accessible to me at that time because I was not connected to my higher conscious self, and the truth of my pre-agreement. The disconnection from my higher self left me in a vulnerable state of confusion as to what my life's learning's was all about? If I'd had access to this important information it would have saved me from some of the pain and grief that I'd created for myself. Life would have been so much easier if I'd known the details about my life lessons before hand, about what would happen to me and the reasons why? It would have allowed me to be more accepting of my life's experiences, making everything within my life all right, and easier to bear.

I pre-agreed to everything that I actually did, and I'd agreed to the events that would happen within this lifetime before I was born. I understood and knew the reasons as to why the different situations or circumstances would be played out, and to how they would affect me. I was also given the solutions to overcome all of my problems, and how to alleviate the imbalances from within my life. I knew the information about my past lifetimes that were relevant to this one, and too why certain things would happen, and also what I had to do, too overcome them.

What had happened to me within this lifetime I'd created anguish or torment for myself and others in another lifetime, and hadn't successfully dealt with the emotional issues or imbalances at the time when I should have? In that lifetime I hadn't learned from my lessons or experiences and upon my death I'd taken the negative vibrations of those learning's onto the next level of my existence, where I would then gain a deeper understanding. The understanding of my learning's would allow me to be accepting of what had happened to me, and then I'd choose another lifetime in order to come back to earth to fully understand and overcome those learning's, so I could release the negativity that I'd created for my soul.

So this is how the soul's journey starts all over again, with the intention of us living our lives, to overcome some important learning's. The details of that agreement or the memories of which, are locked deep within our sub-conscious at the moment of our birth. Waiting until the time becomes right, for us to search for or unlock those memories from deep within our sub-conscious, and then to reconnect with the truth about our true selves. Until then, we have to maintain faith, trust and belief in ourselves, accepting our life's lessons as part of the divine plan.

So for me, in being able to accept my demise was to be a big part of my life's lessons and learning's. So having pre-agreed to all the different aspects of my life, I had to wait for the right time in order for them to be played out, and for me to gain the learning's and in-sight into their true meanings. When we fail to understand what our emotional imbalances are all about, creates the unrest within. Then we risk aliments, illness or disease being created from the hardships within our lives, all because we've held onto the negative imbalance of our miss-perception of what's happened to us.

The journey of self-awareness allowed me to learn so much about myself, realising that who I'd now become was really who I'd always been, but without the negative traits. In other words my higher conscious self and truth without the negative undertones of my learning's, with me only displaying my positive attributes now. With the reconnection of my higher conscious self and truth, I reinstated self-love, faith, belief, and trust, which allows me to understand my life's purpose as it happens and deal with everything positively. I was so joyful to realise that the way I'd allowed my life to unfold, and to the choices and decisions that I'd made, I was supposed to make them, because it was all I'd pre-agreed a long time ago.

The in-sight into the divine plan was quite informative, the reason of what happened to me, I had created for someone else in a previous lifetime but also to understand the emotional trauma I'd created for me had caused me to fall out of love with myself, but now I do love myself, and others unconditionally. So what we give out is what we get back, not always in the same lifetime but when the time becomes right for us to gain a deeper understanding of what we needed to learn in order to evolve.

Thinking that I was hard done too, was just a state of mind, and once I'd healed my life, I could focus on the positive aspects of those learning's. It's about what we do within our lives and the underlying reasons behind them; it's about our hidden agenda, and facing the real reasons behind our insecurities or negative emotions. The unhappiness that I'd created for me was about the lack of faith in me, others, and the bigger picture of my life.

When we realise there is a reason as to why these life experiences happen to us allows us to realise the truth of all things? There is a bigger picture about our lives, and it tells a story of long ago. The answer to my life's lessons was simple; no-one can love me but me, and by not loving me enough caused a state of unhappiness that cost me dearly, but I've understood it was all part of my pre-destined destiny, and the life I choose to live. The lesson learned was, I love myself unconditionally, and the love I'd shared with others still exists. It's an infinite love and it bonds souls together, knowing they are supported by that love till the end of time, and beyond.

The lessons we've not yet learned or overcome, we still have to experience, whether in this lifetime or another. More importantly if we live in truth, light and love, we will conquer our soul's quest now! Remember all we need is within just waiting for us to re-connect with; it's our truth of all things, and all that we need to live our lives successfully, and all that we do, is for the highest good of all.

How do we know what unconditional love feels like? It's the love we feel when we hold a new born baby in our arms for the first time, and especially if they are blood related to us. Now that is a definitive love and it's a love with no hidden agenda or price tag.

CHAPTER 3

THE PROCESS OF SELF-HEALING

Our quest of this lifetime is to become self-aware which allows us to become more spiritually, mentally and physically aware of our many needs. This process takes us on a journey to becoming our true selves once more, by activating our natural gifts, skills, and abilities; in order to self heal on every level of our being. First we have to be honest with ourselves to the possibility that we have imbalances or negativity that's held within the mind, body or soul. When we recognise this we can then seek the help we need to alleviate the discomfort, illness or disease. We can then seek the infinite knowledge and wisdom that would allow us to understand, and overcome any problem or issue consciously.

We must all take responsibility for us because at times we need to seek medical help if we have an illness, disease or condition that needs attention. Conventional medicines, and the alternative approaches to illness or disease go hand in hand, and it's important to heal the mind, body and the soul, on all levels of existence in order for us to achieve a well being state.

Everything that happens to us happens for a reason, even illness and disease. When we understand why we have coughs, colds or even muscular or skeleton problems, heart attacks or diabetes and so on, can tell us a lot about what's going on within our lives. What happens to us outwardly also denotes what's happening to us within. When we understand the coincidences or mirror images of life, we then realise that these are the messages or signals from our higher conscious self telling us all's not well, and we need to overcome our problems, and achieve a well being state once again. When we recognise the warning signs of the unrest of our mind, body or soul, allows us to seek the help or to get the understanding to alleviate the imbalances or negativity that's held within, consciously or sub-consciously.

When I was forty years old, I had migraine headaches that disabled me for anything from twenty-four to seventy-two hours on a regular basis, and over a ten year period. I was on medication but to no avail! So after seeking help through the alternative methods, and on addressing my migraines, I found out that I was controlling the different issues within my life. Once I'd understood the process, I was able to release the negatives, and let go of the controls, alleviating the discomfort, and I haven't had a migraine since. Just by changing our perception to the way we perceive the different situations or circumstances within our lives, allows us to be more accepting of the things that we have no control over. By being accepting of life's experiences can alleviate ailments, illness or even disease as long as we understand what our negative emotions have done to us. We can elevate all discomforts from within our lives, if we are committed to doing so.

If you have a problem that's causing you concern or unrest and maybe contributing to an ailment, illness or imbalance, you need to address or analyze the situation by going within, and asking your higher conscious self a question! What is this ailment, illness or imbalance about? Allow yourself to be truthful with the reply, by recognising that there is a problem, we can then seek help allowing us to overcome our difficulties.

When we listen to our bodies many needs, and by not denying us in anyway, we consider our thoughts, feelings or the need for some rest bite that would allow us the opportunity to heal our lives. We don't always recognise that we have the ability to self-heal, and with a positive mindset we can change the way we feel about certain situations or circumstances within our lives allowing us to achieve well being. This gives us a positive approach to life's challenges, with us overcoming them consciously; we wouldn't have created any negative imbalances for us.

There are a lot of self help books on the market that will allow us to deal with our problems, and overcome difficulties. But the only sure way of getting our lives back on track is the inner journey that connects us to the blueprint of whom we truly are, and where we can successfully access our truth. The journey of self awareness changes lives, and when we are true to us, we can change anything within our lives consciously. When we change our perception or thought patterns, we gain a deeper understanding of our life's purpose and experiences. With the purpose of us all living the life that was intended, instead of the one that's derived from life's struggles and their affects to our minds, body or soul.

To be our truth we have to be totally honest with ourselves, and then a healing takes place. When we know why we have a physical or mental problem we can alleviate the negativity from within in order to recognise our truth about any given situation or circumstance which then aids healing. When we understand the real reasons behind what we do, say or think, we must hear our truth, speak our truth and see our truth, then healing takes place naturally.

The mind is a very complex organ; it gets us into all sorts of trouble without us even knowing it's happened to us, all because of our mindset. When we are negative then negative things happen to us, and when we are positive we can achieve anything we want, as long has it's for the highest good of all. But first, each individual has to change the way they perceive themselves and the situations within their lives, then they can achieve their own inner peace, which eventually contributes towards achieving world peace.

Inner peace happens when we become our truth, we need to heal our lives to achieve that inner peace. We need to stay calm when negative things happen, because in calm we are prepared, and in calm we are protected. If we stay calm in any given negative situation we can activate our truth, in order to find a positive solution to our problem. If we get anxious with any of life's experiences, we lose the connection from within to stay calm. It's about us being of help, and not about adding to the problem by not staying calm. When we are calm, we are connected to our truth, so we can deal successfully with any situation that we find us in. This saves us from taking the trauma or negative imbalances on board and holding them within, thinking that we've failed in some-way or life's treated us harshly and we're being punished.

I was burgled for a second time within an eighteen month period. I tried to stay positive and calm, thinking why had it happened again? Understanding that it was just a part of life's trail's and tribulations, and these negative things do happen, with me trying not to take it personally. By staying calm and in that moment I knew that this time around he would be caught. Then the trauma of what had happen to me, took over and I went through the process of calling the police and insurance company. I dealt with the situation with a calm and positive mindset, finding myself experiences moments of doubt, but overall knowing I had no choice other than to make sure I did what I needed to do, and to overcome this traumatic situation positively.

When I was burgled the first time I'd reacted differently, and the whole process was stressful and traumatic which caused me to lose confidence in me, thinking I was being punished in some-way. I was very nervous and at times afraid to leave my property in case they came back, I became paranoid. In order for me to overcome the ordeal I sought alternative help, and tried to understand why I'd been burgled in the first place, only to find out that I was afraid of loss, because I'd lost everything I'd worked for because of my divorce, so I became a victim yet again. Even though I was burgled a second time it was in order to catch the culprits and justice be done.

Two weeks later the burglars were caught whilst burgling someone else, an item of my jewellery was recovered from their home address that then placed them at my scene also. I felt a tremendous sense of relief that the culprits had been caught, and eventually they were sent to prison. We can't always prevent negative things from happening to us but we can choose to deal with them positively, and allow ourselves to go through the positive unfolding of grief and mourning of any negative situation. By staying calm we can go through the process of any traumatic situation naturally, knowing if we're accepting of all situations we can change the way we feel regardless of the outcome. We can't change what's happened to us, but we do have a choice in how we let it affect us, and by dealing with any situation positively we then avoid any negativity from effecting our mind, body or soul. If the negativity is left untreated it will cause unrest within that we'll have to sort out at a later date.

When we experience the tragic loss of a loved one, we go through a period of total shock where the mind closes down, protecting the body and soul. When we have recovered sufficiently we can pick up the pieces, and try to deal with the situation knowing that God always sends people to help us through our difficult times. We can then draw on their strength and courage, in order to overcome our ordeal regardless of how long it takes us. This allows us to be more accepting of what's happened to us, so we can then pick up the pieces, and rebuild our lives. We cannot change what happens to us but we can choose how we deal with it.

We can set ourselves free when we understand and accept that we do have a choice in how we let things affect us, and this allows us to overcome any of life's experiences which makes us stronger, but also redefines who we are. The blueprint of who we are holds the secrets that allow us to overcome the trails and tribulations of our life's purpose, allowing us to achieve our potential. Our potential is the positive attributes of who we really are, but more importantly what we've achieved or accomplished.

We are the crusaders of all lifetimes, with us living our lives to the full, and understanding that there nothing that we cannot overcome as long as we have determination, commitment and courage. We have done it all before, and overcome it all before but in other lifetimes; this life is about honouring all lives, and by being our truth we can successfully conquer all.

Whilst experiencing life's struggles and hardships they'll teach us how to show compassion and understanding to all, and not to judge ourselves or others. We must treat us with consideration and kindness, because of our hidden agendas that we're working too! When we recognise our lessons, we can help others to understand theirs, because life is about us all helping the other to overcome the hard times. When we help each other it makes our suffering easier to bear and overcome, as life can be really lonely at times, and especially if we feel deserted or abandoned.

At times we often crave support but because we are deluded to our true feelings, we don't always allow others to help us, and we dismiss their help because we're too proud or hurt to let them. I'd done just that, and by telling others I was okay they believed me, when the truth was I was not okay has I was struggling with my life and needed help, compassion, and support. So I continued to struggle, and few years later I realised that I needed help, because my perception was that I thought it was a weakness to admit defeat or to acknowledge that I wasn't coping, and when I asked for help people willingly gave it.

At times we all need help and support as we struggle with life, and occasionally other people's kindness can reduce us to tears. It's important that we help each other because we stand more chance of recognising our true feelings or emotions which allows us to be totally honest with us. We then realise that we're not alone in our suffering or hardships, as everyone struggles with the different aspect of their lives at sometime or other. We do not have to go on a spiritual journey in order to overcome our problems or issues, as long as we just recognise we have a problem, because then we stand more chance of overcoming them together.

At times we bury our heads in the sand, hoping that our problems will go away, and at times they do. The deeper rooted problems will manifest themselves over and over again, with us becoming disheartened or discouraged until we do sort them. We have to have commitment and faith in order to overcome our problems but when it's right for us to do so, until then we must be accepting of what has happened or happening to us, by staying positive in order to override the storm or challenges, with us succeeding in all we do.

Some people go through life oblivious to their problems and that's okay but what they have to realise is, that at sometime or other they will have to address their issues or problems. This is in order to achieve well being state because we all want to live a long and healthy life, and we can only do this if we're aware of the unrest or imbalance within. Sometimes we find ourselves having a conversation with someone, and we have a revelation about some aspect or other within our lives because of what's been said. Everything we need comes to us in order to learn from, as long as we're open to receiving it.

At times the understanding of what we're doing is all that's needed for us to learn, and we can continue to learn from each other through the art of communication because then we'd learn instantly. We owe it to us to be mindful of the outside influences in life, whether negatively or positively because looking at the bigger picture of life, allows us to stay in control of our true destiny with our life's purpose unfolding naturally and positively.

With life's synchronicities and the many coincidences, we are all given the opportunity to recognise our imbalances or disharmonious situations within our lives, but also to help one another through the different processes of overcoming our problems no matter what they are. Everyone who's in our lives is in them for a reason. We attract all that we need in order to learn from, and the biggest teachings come from our families and friend, as like attracts like. If I'm angry at someone, the

23

mirror image is I'm angry at me and hadn't recognised that fact or if I'm disappointed with someone, it's really me I'm disappointed at, maybe I'd let me down by not fulfilling my promise or obligation to me. We can learn so much from the mirror images of us or the synchronicities and coincidences, because these are the messages or signs that we seek in answer to our dilemmas within our lives.

The process of self healing is to be self-aware, body-aware and spiritually-aware, in order for us to heal every aspect of our lives, but more importantly to be consciously aware of what we are doing, saying, thinking or manifesting. Life is a great adventure, and it's important that we all live our lives to the full whilst achieving our dreams or goals.

CHAPTER 4

MY JOURNEY

My story begins when I was 45 years old and living in a beautiful cottage in a small village in Norbury, Staffordshire. I had just spent the last two years living on a narrow-boat enjoying the waterways at 4mph whilst recovering from the divorce of my first husband. It was very therapeutic to be at one with nature, and it helped with my healing process after a very traumatic time. I became more spiritually aware by reading self help books and also experiencing the alternative approaches to life, so spirituality became a way of life and it wasn't long before I began to pick up the pieces of my new life!

It was lovely to be back on land, and to have more room to entertain my family and friends. The surrounding country side was breathe taking, and just a short walk to the canal where I could still enjoy the tranquility of the waterways. I would walk for hours along the towpath watching the boats as they meandered by. I wanted the best of both worlds really, to still own a boat whilst living in the cottage, and having lived on a narrow boat, and travelled the waterways I had lots of special memories, and I continued to live the dream by watching others enjoy the same experience. I always found that the community on the waterways to be very friendly and the people were very supportive of each other.

Whilst I was living on the narrow boat I found myself a job working for a boat builder, making the soft furnishings for the boats that he built, and occasionally I would varnish the woodwork. My life was beginning to settle down after the ordeal of my divorce, but I still wondered why it had all happened in the first place? Because I had married for life, so it was a big shock to find myself a divorcee.

Three years after my divorce I fell in-love for the second time in my life, to the boat builder I worked for. It was a whirlwind courtship, and I soon found myself walking down the aisle six months later. My new husband brought spontaneity into my life, showing me how easy it was to just go with the flow of life, without the need to anchor myself down with the many responsibilities that I'd often placed upon myself. I realised how I'd made me responsible for so many things in the past, no wonder I'd put myself under too much pressure and struggled with my life. Often telling me that I couldn't do this, that or the other, giving a hundred reasons as to why, which kept me locked into my comfort zone. So for me it was a big wakeup call to just go with the flow of life, and to see where life took me.

Life had become exciting again as I now experienced new skills helping my husband with building and selling boats. We started to travel abroad looking for fibreglass boat in order to offer a wider range of boats, and not just selling steel barges. We enjoyed travelling with us eventually settling down to live in Ireland where we continued to build and sell boats, and started a boat hire company for the Irish tourists. I still felt the unrest within me, and at time felt I'd run away from my unhappiness that I still felt. I tried hard to settle into my new life but I missed my family back home in the UK.

My marriage to my second husband was about us both healing from past trauma, but sadly we were not able to maintain a happy equilibrium, due to the emotional issues that we both hadn't dealt with from previous relationships. At that point I'd not dealt with the breakdown of my first marriage, so sadly our marriage came to an end, so at the age of 49 years I found myself going back home to my family.

After the breakdown of my second marriage, I was so distraught; it made me take an even closer look at myself. I felt I hadn't learned anything has regards to my personal life, because I was experiencing an emotional state of failure, feeling suicidal again, and having the strong emotions of defeat. Not realising at the time that the program I had still running within, was one of denial of my emotional and physical being, and I felt that I was not destined to be truly happy; I had survived one broken marriage, could I survive a second? I retreated again back to nature in order to heal my wounded spirit.

The journey that followed was hard, because I felt that I would never be able to comprehend what had happened to me or even to understand why? I really did not know what I'd done to warrant the situation or circumstances that I found myself in, yet again. So my inner journey started, because I felt I was incapable of making any positive choices or decisions within my life because I felt a failure or so I thought. To my surprise I found the courage to keep moving forwards, but it's very difficult when you don't really trust your instincts or decisions. We all at times do what we have too in maintaining an outer show of confidence, whilst experiencing inner turmoil.

My inner journey allowed me to analyze my feelings, as to why I couldn't find true happiness, even though I still felt I was being punished in some-way. I always thought myself to be kind and considerate of others, so why was I struggling so much with my personal life? I decided to experience the different holistic technique, and their alternative approaches in aiding well being that would allow me to understand my present situation and circumstances.

At first I had to be totally honest with myself about how I felt within. I knew I'd pressed myself self-destruct years earlier because of my suicidal tendencies, so I needed to know why? I felt un-loveable, despondency and gloom, and with no self-worth or esteem. I had very little confidence in me, and hated how my life had turned out. So I retreated even more within myself, watching other succeed but my life was on hold with me not moving forwards. I was in a stalemate situation; I was dammed if I did, and dammed if I didn't.

I was struggling with my life with me just going through the motions of my daily chores, and I justified why I wasn't achieving by working hard for others to succeed because I didn't believe in me anymore. I seemed to spend the next few years just living in the shadow of my former self, always looking back to some idyllic time when I felt life was happier. I wanted my life back with my first husband but I was in denial of my feelings or should I say, I wouldn't allow myself to acknowledge my true feelings so I kept them suppressed for years.

I was living my life but not in my truth, and at that particular time I was not aware of what my true feelings were all about. I experienced and enjoyed lots of different aspects of my life, seeing my children find partners and get married, and start their own families. My children and grandchildren brought me immense joy, and we had lots of great times together but my personal life was still on hold, even though I hadn't recognised that as being so at the time. My unhappiness was growing, and I was creating even more unrest within my mind, body and soul.

My spiritual journey continued in order for me to experience a lot of different holistic techniques, and gain the understanding their unique benefits. I went through the process of elevating the imbalances or disharmony from within, and I tried to understand what the unhappiness was all about? Very slowly my life started to move forwards, but I felt immense sadness within, and this was to be my mindset for years to come, all because I was in denial of how I still felt about my first husband. I had told myself over the years that I didn't love him, because of what happened between us. I'd thought I'd fallen out of love with him, when in fact I'd fallen out of love with myself; this was quite a revelation in my spiritual journey and growth, because I could now focus on seeking my truth about what happened between us, and it was the truth that would eventually set me free.

One day as I was sitting at the kitchen table just finishing my breakfast, enjoying the sun has it shone through the window; I suddenly had this overwhelming feeling of love. I wasn't even sure what I'd been thinking about, but I suddenly realised I was still in love with my first husband, and the revelation was! He was still the love of my life, I felt so happy because I'd never fallen out of love with him, only me. As I continued to sit there thinking of my journey of self awareness, I realised that I'd never really loved myself, and I'd been searching for a love that only I could give myself. In that moment I realised that I'd not fully understood the consequence of not loving myself enough, and to the affects it had on my mind, body and soul was unbelievable, let alone my personal life.

The realisation that I'd also had very little self-belief, faith or trust in me became evident, and I wasn't even sure that I'd ever really loved myself at all, only to discover this was what my life's purpose had been all about. I'd been searching for a love that only I could give myself, and it was a journey that had started years earlier with my grandmother, who didn't seem to like me. Over the years I tried my best to get her to like me, and I now realised I'd been doing the same ever since not just with my grandmother but all who came into my life. I did this by giving too much of myself to others thinking it would buy me their love, only it didn't.

My parents must have been beside themselves at times because looking back I was a child that always craved attention. I wasn't demanding but I was always in trouble, putting myself in the front line for photographs or dancing and singing just to let everyone know I was around. I always thought I was a free spirit and enjoyed life, but now I can see what I was lacking, and how I was reacting in order to get recognition, attention or love. My parents often told me that little girls should be seen and not heard, but I had an inquisitive mind, and I wanted to know why things happened all the time. It was twenty questions in as many minutes, I'm sure they loved me really! At last my life's purpose and understanding had presented itself to me, but I felt I'd wasted an awful lot of time learning this valuable lesson, and it had cost me dearly.

The understanding of searching for self-love is the greatest gift anyone can give themselves because it opens many doors to achieving our potential, and allows life to deliver the many opportunities that we've dismiss over the years all because of the unrest within us. The majority of us at sometime or other will have experienced no self-love or very little self-love. There are lots of reasons as to why we fall out of love with us, and for me I actually came into this life to understand why I would experience a lack of self-love and low self-esteem, and that was the purpose of my life in order to gain the understanding and the importance of self-love.

My father often told me that the money he'd spent on my education was wasted but I disagree, because with him telling me that made me work even harder to prove him wrong, as well as my grandmother, and years later I did! I have had a happy and successful life, and because of my hidden agenda of my life's learning's, I'd perceived my life wrongly at times all because of my insecurities, and life's experiences that left me struggling. All of my life's experiences good or bad were pre-destined, to see if I could learn and overcome them, and then to gain the valuable learning's that would set me free from the restraints and restrictions that I'd allowed to happen in order for me to survive my every-day life and realise my full potential and truth.

My life has always been rich with love and support, I'd just perceived it wrongly at times because of my life's experiences, would I change anything? No not really, but maybe the way I had allowed myself to perceive my life's events the way I had, because of the way it had affected me. If I'd have know what my hidden agenda or life's purpose was all about, I would have been more accepting of the experiences I'd had, good or bad.

Hindsight is a wonderful thing but now I know what my life's learning's were all about, I can go on to teach others who want to learn theirs sooner rather than later, because then we'd all save us from a lot of pain or grief, and more importantly time. Because then, we would have more time to enjoy what we already have within our lives, but to enjoy them whole heartily, healthily and wisely. This is the life that our creator intended for us all, but only after completing the first part of our soul's quest in order to overcome our life's purpose, and continue the journey of the soul to achieving ascension.

All that we need is deep within us just waiting for us to stop travelling in an outwards pursuit in search of what we think we need or is missing from within our lives, because we waste too much time. When we reconnect with our unique self that's within we will access our true vibration that's held within the blueprint of who we really are. My spiritual journey and the use of various holistic technique has now transformed my life, and with the New Age of Aquarius will allow us all to activate what we need almost instantly by being our truth and higher conscious self.

It's the truth that eventually sets us free, but also in understanding that our levels of truth alters almost daily has we learn, and overcome our life's purpose and lessons. The truth of our higher conscious self is a great achievement but the truth of our ascended self is mind blowing and limitless.

CHAPTER 5

JOURNEY OF SELF DISCOVERY

The journey of self discovery and the rebirth of the new you, can be a very exciting and rewarding time. It would have been so much easier if we'd been born with an instruction manual on how to live our lives successfully, tucked beneath our arm. When we understand the agreement we pre-made of what would happen to us, and the choices we could make along the way, we then acquire the ability to overcome any situation or circumstance that we've found ourselves experiencing. Once we've gained the understanding, and have overcome our problems or issues, we would naturally become more attuned to our higher conscious self, where we easily access the information we need in order to have a prosperous, and rewarding life.

Unfortunately upon our birth and due to world vibration the promises and agreements that we made to us was erased from our conscious mind and stored with our sub-conscious. We them have a lifetime to live, with our lives being influenced by an unseen force or vibration duly called our hidden agenda or purpose. Our life's purpose starts to unfold from the moment we can talk and walk, and by the age of five we're well on the way to being influenced by everything and everyone around us, with all that we need in order to fulfil our agreement.

We travel many pathways trying to find what we feel is missing within our lives, but not always knowing what is missing? We all need to be loved, appreciated and cared for, and to have a sense of belonging. We look to other at times to fulfil our many needs because life's experiences can cause us to lose our way or disconnect from our higher conscious self that holds the hidden secrets and messages of our true self, worth, and destiny that would help us solve our own problems or issues. We are all on the journey of our soul's quest in order to fulfil our promises that we made to us long ago. We promised to overcome our problems in order to provide for our own needs, emotionally, physically or mentally.

There is no time scale to the journey of self-discovery as long as we recognise its potential and take that journey when we're ready, and understand the importance to our continued growth, physically, mentally, and spiritually, in-fact on all levels of existence. Everything that happens to us was meant to happen, and there is nothing that we cannot overcome with determination, conviction, and courage. All pathways will lead us to where need to go; we don't find ourselves within the different journeys but through them, by defining our characters and recognising who we really are, with the self-discovery of our truth once more.

We are now living in an age where spirituality is becoming more of a way of life; we do not find ourselves within the spiritual phenomena but with the use and connection of our spiritual gifts, skills, and abilities. To be spiritual is to reconnect with your true soul or essence, trusting in your own abilities and that you're unique. You will then become intuitive, and when you listen to your gut reactions they will let you know right from wrong, and when we listen to our sixth sense of our knowing thoughts, we then make decisions confidently. These are our natural gifts, skills and abilities, and they differ in each and every-one of us, as they do from lifetime to lifetime, all being a part of our continued growth, and the understanding of the integration of all aspect of our unique self.

When we integrate with all aspects of us it's in order to embrace the power within. We will then be more accepting of every aspect of our lives, regardless of what's happened to us. We then understand that the real us, is our higher conscious self and it's always been there, but in the shadows of our lower conscious self. Once we've understood our life's teaching's and when we totally accept the real us, we'll naturally be our higher conscious self. We then take full responsibility for what happens to us because we'll be accepting, and we'll no longer blame others because they too have been influenced by their hidden agendas. With compassion, understanding, and non-judgement we'll set us free to be the real us, the truthfully and higher conscious us.

During the journey of self-discovery you will find out so much about your true-self, being very proud of what you've already achieved or accomplished. We all at sometimes or other behave badly because of our insecurities or unhappiness but it's recognising that good does come from bad if we're willing to learn, and amend our ways. There is nothing that cannot be forgiven in time, because time is a great healer.

God doesn't judge us, we do and each other, and at times unfairly. We are all working to our hidden agendas, in-fact nobody is wrong in what they do, we just consider each other to be wrong. If we can accept all that happens to us it would save us all from pain and grief. What I have understood from my journey of self-discovery was what other did to me rightly or wrongly I'd done to others at sometime or other, whether in this life or another lifetime long ago. That's why we must never judge others because we've all got things wrong at sometime or other.

Every-one of us has a wealth of knowledge and wisdom but as we learn and understand from life's experiences, we'll gain an even greater understanding of what life is really all about, then that knowledge and wisdom becomes infinite, all because we've tapped into the collective consciousness of mankind, and the universal energy of our creator. Our understanding of any knowledge is in the calibration of our level of consciousness, and that level of consciousness changes all the time. We've had other lifetimes where our level of consciousness was higher than it is within this lifetime, and other lifetimes where it was a lot lower. Within this lifetime our level of consciousness was set at our birth, with the potential of us eventually attaining the higher level of consciousness once we've understood our life's journey and connected with our truth in order to continue on our ascended journey.

I have now attained my pre-agreed level of consciousness, and I can look forward to further growth as I continue to learn, and gain even greater understanding of life's experiences that will take me beyond my limitations, and allow me to reach my limitless potential of all lifetimes. I am looking forward to the future, and embracing this golden age of opportunity and growth. I don't know what's beyond this level of conscious growth or to what our limitless potential could be or lead us, but I am excited and feel it beyond even my wildest dreams of chance, growth and opportunity.

Prosperity awaits us all but first it's about the cleansing and purification of our sub-conscious and conscious minds, setting us free from our limiting belief's to embrace a world of great phenomena. The journey of self-discovery is a journey of the self back to the self; it's about reinventing and rediscovering our authentic self, allowing us to empower our true-self, transforming our life, and all lives consciously. This is the journey of the soul's quest, and it's potentially an exciting journey of self discovery!

We discovery many things about us realising that we are the person we've always aspired too, but as the higher conscious us we realise how simple are lives can be now that we have faith, belief and trust in us to accomplish all that we desire, with us no longer giving our power away by thinking someone else knows better than us about the different aspects of our lives. We have to hold our vision and dreams until we have brought them into fruition, knowing that the process is all part of achieving our goals and allows us to live in the now enjoying all that we do consciously.

What I've understood whilst going through my journey of self discovery was even though the process was hard work for me at times, it was because of the teachings I could share with others. In understanding the process that we go through to achieve a higher conscious state, I'd understood how hard we make our lives because we hadn't understood the consequence of what our miss-perceptions was in fact doing to us emotionally, physically or even mentally which had an overall effect on our soul.

When helping others, and once they've acknowledged there's a problem or issue within that needs understanding in order to overcome it, just to acknowledge the truth about what it's all about, allows an instant healing to occur. This creates a shift in our consciousness that allows us to experience other situations within our lives just the same, easily and effortlessly. The higher our consciousness rises, the more in-tune we are to ourselves and others, with us being able to see a bigger picture of our life, which gives us compassion and understanding to others, as well as us.

Our higher consciousness will reactivate our gifts, skills and abilities naturally. This is happening because the world vibration is lifting with the purification and cleansing of not just our world but us also. This process allows us to confidently address all situations within our lives in truth, where we can let go of our negative emotions and the imbalances within all aspects of our lives. It the truth in all things that set us free from our restraints and restriction that we've held us to because of our insecurities.

Life is about doing less and achieving more, so let us do ourselves a favour by not complicating things by being ignorant to our disharmonies or unrest within, because once we've recognised and released them, we are free to be the best we can be. We then have a fulfilling and rewarding life in order to share our good fortune with others, with us all giving to the other, unconditionally.

CHAPTER 6

LIMITING BELIEF'S

Our limiting beliefs stop us from making positive decisions about our lives, and then taking action into achieving our dreams, goals or desires. Our beliefs are what we perceive to be true by the mind that influences our body or soul. When a belief as been accepted by us as being true, it becomes a program which then limits us. But not all of our beliefs are true, they are what we want to perceive as being true because of situations or circumstances within our lives, as it allows us to cope and feel good about us even though it's short lived.

These beliefs or programs are called illusions, and has us deluding the self; into thinking we're okay when in fact we're clearly not. Illusions are our way of coping with the different issues or situations within our lives that we're not happy with, but thinking that we don't have a choice so therefore can't change them. These illusions help us to deal with what's going on within our everyday lives, and our emotions play an important part in the way we perceive the different situations or circumstances. Our emotions can get the better of us which can cause us to be slightly out of balance or unreasonable in our expectations of what we want to achieve, and to the desired outcome being influenced by our insecurities. This is when we're not being our truth, with us kidding ourselves to what really going on.

The emotional issues within our lives create physical or mental imbalances which stops us from accessing the solution to our problems. Common sense often evades us because the answer to the problem is out of proportion to the solution, things often seem worse than what they really are. Out of our emotional anguish we allow ourselves to become temporarily blinded by what we need to be real in order to function within our daily lives. Justifying our needs or wants with us being totally oblivious to the truth of what's really going on within our lives, can and does often allow us to be deluded. We cannot justify our truth only our untruths as these are our limiting beliefs that will keep us struggling with our lives.

Our hidden agendas has us travelling many pathways in life, and sometimes blindly, with us hoping that things turn out the way we hoped for or with any luck we get things right with very little effort on our part, only to find they're short lived. At times our emotions get the better of us out of desperation or frustration, and we often make others or even the different situations within our lives a projection of our insecurities. We focus on them because it distracts us from ourselves, and with us not having to sort our issues out. Not realising the illusions within our lives, and to what they are all about? With us only seeing what we want to see, by dismissing the unrest within our soul, and by telling us we're okay when in fact we're not!

Our emotional insecurities create the illusions from our negative emotions such as; rejection, feeling lonely or desertion, resentment or betrayal, in fact any negative emotion that leaves us questioning, self doubting or procrastinating because we have regrets! We create illusions because of our mechanism of self preservation, only seeing what we want to see, in order to cope with what's going on within our lives, often keeping us locked into our comfort zones. We often protect us from life's issues that are going to hurt us or make us justify the things we do.

Our limiting beliefs feeds our protective fears that disables us from achieving what we desire or we end up breaking the promises that we've made to us, because we've become disillusioned with our lives. When we don't fulfil our promises to us, we then focus on others instead, with us helping them to succeed because we don't want to let them down, but often letting us down in the process. This leaves us feeling frustrated or disappointed, and often angry with us, which leaves us feeling despondent or unhappy and we then procrastinate the self. We are our hardest critics because we don't show us compassion or understanding.

So what is a limiting belief? It's a negative belief or fear that we can't achieve what we want to accomplish, with us putting restraints, restrictions and obstacles in our way to justify the lack of effort on our part or as to why things have not materialised the way we hoped for. In fact any excuse as to why we can't achieve what we have pre-agreed too. We often desire things within our lives not always for the right reason, and by not achieving them cause's unrest within. It takes a lot of courage to be honest with us, and admit we may be wrong in the reasons why we want certain things within our lives, all because we needed to pacify the unrest within.

At sometime or other we all do things we're not proud of, with us justifying our actions, thoughts, and judgements of us, and then others. So when we change the way we perceive the different aspects of our lives we can then alter our mindsets to being more positive, and we take responsibility for us and our actions no longer justifying what we do. We then gain more confidence, and have courage, focus, and commitment in achieving our dreams or goals realistically. Our limiting beliefs are our insecurities of self doubt, self punishment, no self-worth, belief, faith, trust or love, and low self-esteem. When we pay no attention to our intuition or knowing thoughts of our higher conscious self we create the imbalances within, instead of allowing us to be gently guided forwards by our higher consciousness.

All illusions of life are about our perception of what we think is happening within our lives, We all view these perceptions differently that's why it's important to ask for help or advice because we can all help each other into finding a more appropriate solution to our problems, a problem shared is a problem halved, as two heads are better than one. Some of us see it as a weakness to ask for help, and often struggle for years until we recognise that we do need help because we're really struggling, and that we have to give us permission to seek that help. At times we become so stubborn we often deny us help or to recognise that we do in fact need help.

Every-one of us needs to feel needed or we crave support with us thinking nobody cares or is even aware of our problems. When we ask for help others gladly offer that help, but at times we're so out of balance that we refuse that help for all sorts of reasons and often spiting ourselves in the process. By refusing help we deny us because we hadn't recognised the fact that we needed help. We have to let others help us from time to time, maybe they needed to help us for them to feel a part of our lives or to repay us for what we've already done for them. This process reinstates caring for each other, and a willingness to help those who are struggling to help themselves. There's a big lesson for us all to learn here! In understanding that we're all part of the family of life, and it's important to help one another because it promotes compassion and understanding in us all, and allows us not to judge when we don't understand others situations or problems.

Our pride and ego can play a big part in deluding us, and creates our limiting beliefs or programs. Sometimes we become set in our ways, and can get blinkered with us not being able to recognise the real truth of any given situation. We can often be stubborn, refusing to let others help us by not bending a little, all because we've become too rigid in our ways of thinking and doing, and our pride plays a big part in us denying us help. We then think we know what's right, when in fact someone else can contribute to a more complete solution or idea. Our peripheral vision can be very limiting; we need to push those boundaries out, allowing our minds energy to expand, and be more open and accepting to other possibilities, with us achieving a successful outcome for all.

When we justify our actions we are basically trying to convince others and ourselves that we're right, when in fact we're saying that we may be wrong in some way! We then end up giving our power away, which robs us of our confidence, self assurance, and then we become confused with us saying I don't know any more, you choose. This gives others power over us and it's not long before we live our lives through them because we've become confused with us, by not knowing what we want any more. When this happens it leaves us yearning or desiring something that we're not prepared to achieve in fear of failure, rejection or simply because we think we're out of our depth by saying I can't do this, that or the other, when in fact we can choose to achieve what we want.

Our limiting beliefs are part of the programmed us and also our life's purpose or lessons. We need to overcome these limiting beliefs in order to set us free, by learning the important facts about the real us, and our delusions.

The number one illusion is in thinking that we're hard done too, and therefore we become a victim.

The second is to think we're being punished for a crime we've not committed, albeit not necessarily in this lifetime but trust me we have in other lifetime that's why we must never judge others, and by overcoming our purpose will set us free.

The third is to allow us to stay ignorant to the possibility that by not being our truth we are deluding us, and when we take responsibility to being our truth, we then realise we've always had a choice in all that we've ever done, good or bad. No one as every made us do anything we haven't wanted to do, because no one held a gun to our heads and made us do anything that we didn't want to do, no one that is but us! So the decisions we've made, we choose to make them for whatever reason, and in understanding the truth behind that reason will set us free from us from the restraints and restriction that we've allowed to stop us from achieving our dreams or goals.

All of our limiting beliefs come from the lower conscious us; we make those beliefs consciously, based on what's happening within our lives and too how we've perceived them.

We then accept the belief as being real by the mind, that influences the body as being true, and over a period of time those illusions become a sub-conscious program. These programs run sub-consciously until we reawaken to what's happening to us or basically until we've have had enough heartache, struggles and disappointments within our lives, and consciously we try to understand our problem so we can overcome them and move onto better things.

Some programmes can work to our benefit or detriment depending on what the program is, and to how we react to them. Most people live all of their lives oblivious to the programs that are running. Some of us bring these programs into this lifetime with us, all being part of our life's purpose, lessons or experiences that we need in order to learn from and evolve. These negative or limiting programs can have us self sabotaging our efforts, and at times can have us on a self destruct pathway or we hold ourselves back from what we want to achieve because of some underlying fear, and we have no clue as to what the fear is all about.

Our thoughts are created by our experiences, and our experiences are created by our perception of what's going on at the time, but also what's happening to us personally or emotionally. Limiting beliefs are sometimes handed down to us through the different generations of what they considered to be right.

With each generation comes new advanced technology and trends, and the younger generation are in danger of only focusing on things outside of themselves because of all the distractions within our world of technology, and the brain washing of how others influence our lifestyles. This can be a problem because of our unrealistic demands; our perception of what we consider to be real confuses us.

We can so easily lose touch with reality, especially if we feel emotional or insecure. It's important to make major decisions when we feel confident and calm, and we're realistic in the goals we set ourselves. We can at times take on to much, putting ourselves under too much pressure which just adds to the confusion. We must be honest with us when making decisions or choices because anything but the truth of what we do will influences the outcome.

Our potential is limitless, so we mustn't allow our limiting beliefs stop us from achieving a successful life. If we want to be successful in all that we do, it starts with the journey of the higher conscious self, to an enlightened journey of ascension which sets us free from our limiting beliefs and fears.

My limiting beliefs had stopped me from achieving over the years, with my negative thoughts, and others were programs that I had running all brought on by my negative mindset of thinking I couldn't achieve, with me giving myself a valid reason as to why. Only later on I understood that some of my limiting beliefs were often fear based, and on addressing those negative beliefs I found I was lacking in confidence, courage or conviction.

Depending on what's happened to us through life's experiences it's important that we empower us to succeed and not to give into our limiting beliefs. I often found myself pushing others forwards to achieve their dreams or goals because I was afraid to push me forwards in order to become successful in what I did, because I didn't believe in myself enough. People looking at me would think I'm a confident person, which to some degree I am but because of my insecurities I'd allowed my limiting beliefs to stop me from achieving my dreams or goals.

Now I achieve all that I desire consciously because I'm aware that from time to time I'll still have doubts about what I want to achieve, but if I'm perfectly honest with me I can push aside any setbacks, and move forwards in earnest to achieve my goals. It is the truth of all things that sets us free!

CHAPTER 7

EMPOWER THE MIND, BODY & SOUL

The power of the soul is the realisation and activation of our unrealised limitless potential. We cannot achieve this potential until we have successfully reconnected to our infinite power within, as this is the power of our truth. When we fully understand what our life's purpose and experiences have been all about, will release the emotional and negative imbalances that are held within?

Whilst experiencing all aspects of life, we will always have negative issues or circumstances to understand and overcome which often leaves us with emotional issues. We must recognise these emotional imbalances as they happen to us, and then let go of the negative undertones, and only keep the positive learning's and experience. The most important time is the now, so we owe it to us to achieve what we need to achieve today, and not put them off until another time. It is important that we only concentrate on the now where we can let our day to day life unfold naturally, with us projecting and attracting all that we desire positively.

With our reconnection to the power within we need to maintain a strong connection to the source using the power everyday in everyway. It is important that we truly believe in miracles, and that they really do happen, because if we don't believe in miracles, we will block us from receiving what we truly desire. Miracles are preformed everyday, just think about it! What have you achieve in your life against all odds, maybe thinking that you wouldn't achieve it or have you had a near miss in a car that you were travelling in? Are you and your family healthy and striving? As someone you know just given birth or recovered from an illness or disease against all odds? Have you just landed yourself a dream job or met the partner of your dreams? All of these are miracles.

When we are connected to the power of our soul, we can manifest all that we desire. We must be aware of our thoughts because even our negative thoughts will manifest, so we must be very careful only to have positive thoughts. If I find myself having a negative thought I immediately say cancel that! And replace with a positive thought. The Law of Attraction already affects our daily lives, so make sure it's in a positive way. What do you need right now? Ask yourself and be honest as to the reason why you want this, that or the other, because we have to have pure intention. If we have any doubts about what we are trying to manifest, we will not be able to manifest successfully or achieve a positive outcome.

I had a friend who once asked if she could perform a miracle for me and asked what I wanted. She told me to be pure in what I asked for, and to have a clear intention of why I wanted it. The truth was, when she put me on the spot I honestly didn't know what I wanted, where has before she asked everything I thought I wanted I now realised was quite superficial. This is about being truthful with us as to what we really want, and not what we think we want, because there's a huge difference between the two!

In order to manifest we need to empower our mind, body and soul, re-educating us to become a powerful being once more, because when we're having a good day everything goes smoothly and we can manifest what we want, but on a bad day the world seems to be against us. There is a simple technique that I use to keep my energy and vibration positive, and helps to keep my connection with the higher vibration strong, in order to achieve and become successful in all that I do. This technique is a tapping to the rhythm of your own vibration. If you tap with your right hand onto the back of your left arm, just let yourself feel your body's own natural rhythm. Does it feel slow, medium or is it a fast rhythm?

If the rhythm is slow you may be feeling depressed and hadn't recognised that fact, and if it's medium then you're feeling down or fed up because at times we get bored with what we're doing. If your rhythm is fast then you feel quite upbeat and happy. So let's look at the slow or medium rhythm, I want you to think of happier times within your life, and then empower yourself by tapping to that upbeat rhythm, the faster it is the more you empower you to be energised and vibrant. Now think about your life in the present and tap to the faster rhythm, straight away your vibration will be uplifted, you will feel empowered by the new thought of being happy and contented. But more importantly you'll feel confident in whatever task you're aiming to do in the present time, with you being influenced by a positive vibration in order to succeed in the goals you've set yourself.

You can do this technique with any different scenario, say you are going to work, and you feel lethargic, and not looking forward to going, tap your arm for your vibration and it's will properly be slow? Well tap again only this time think of the time you enjoyed your work and felt fulfilled, you should be tapping to the faster rhythm. Now think in the present sense and tap to the faster rhythm, straight away you will feel uplifted, and empowered about going to work. Say you have a meeting or interview to go too, and you are suffering from a lack of confidence, tap your arm and if the rhythm is slow or medium think of a time when you were confident, and then re-tap to the faster rhythm empowering yourself with confidence in the now.

Tapping to the rhythm of your bodies' vibration will allow you to understand if you are feeling down, and you hadn't realised that fact. You can tap your vibration at any time in order to empower your rhythm with the strong emotions of encouragement, determination, strength or confidence and for you to be successful with your meeting with the bank manager, prospective employer and so on. The possibilities are huge as to what you can achieve by empowering you. Just think of the technique as the rhythm of life, and you're now dancing your way to success.

Do you ever wonder what your full potential could feel like let alone your limitless one? With you thinking you could never reach your potential as there are too many obstacles in your way. So how do we attain our full potential maybe feeling time is running out before we've embraced the opportunities in order to achieve our potential? The solution is to embrace your limitless potential by meeting your twin soul in another dimension. These twin souls are the entrepreneurs of us in another incarnate form, a successful us, a millionaire us, an artist us or even the writer us. The technique that I use to connect with my twin selves is called quantum connection.

All I do is embrace my power within, and connect with the collective power of the universe and the creator. Then I ask which ever twin that I would like to meet to come and join me in the dimensional place that's connected to the creator's energy. I ask my twin self to inspire me, and to give me advice on what I want to achieve, and then thanking them, allowing myself to come back into this dimension bring the vibration of what I want to accomplish with me. It's important to act on the information given, you may not know straight away what was said but start practicing the gift, skills or talent that you want to achieve and you have asked for. You will be amazed by the outcome, and to what you can naturally accomplish if you put your mind to it.

In simplistic terms all I am doing is connecting with my potential self that was successful in another lifetime, and I bring the vibration of success into this present time, the positive vibrations of those gifts, skills or abilities that I've already accomplished, with me being able to use them to the best of my ability within this lifetime, and for the highest good of all. This is my unrealised potential and it's limitless, and it's all held with the collective consciousness of the real self, and that of our truth!

The power of the soul is infinite; when we reconnect to this power of divinity our potential is limitless. When we understand the law of attraction and abundance we prosper in all that we do, this gives us health, wealth and happiness. We empower us and inspire us to achieve things beyond our wildest dreams, the more we achieve the more knowing we become, acquiring the infinite knowledge and wisdom.

We can manifest all that we desire, and by using our intuition and higher conscious skills more clearly, will enable us to predict our futures successfully. We then activate our kundalini energy, the evolutionary energy that allows us to evolve to higher vibrational levels whilst still here on the earth plane. We also enjoy the life that was intended for us a long time ago. But before we can claim that life, we have to earn the respect, and honour and appreciate the infinite power of the universal energy that allows us to overcome our lessons in life, successfully and easily.

When we empower ourselves with positive affirmations aids us to become successful in all we do, achieving our dreams or goals consciously. Empowered affirmations reignite our sub-conscious in to conscious thinking and action. We empower us even though we sometimes self-doubt or have a lack of self-belief, faith or trust in us and our abilities. The power of positive affirmations has a profound effect on the mind, body and soul, and allows us to re-program old thoughts patterns and beliefs. We then alter our perception about the different situations or circumstances within our lives, making us more accepting to what has happened to us good or bad. When we accept what we can't change, we will have the wisdom to know what we can.

When we recite affirmations and connect with our higher conscious self, allows us to re-educate us into becoming more self-aware, and when we listen to our bodies many needs we then become more body-aware. Affirmations are positive statements that we recite to us, commanding a new belief system within which alters our state of consciousness. We then become more positive about the different thing within our lives which give us the focus and confidence to achieve and accomplish all we desire.

An affirmation is a promise that we make to us to change our thought process into being more positive, with our knowing thoughts promoting action which gives us conviction in all we do. This allows us to continue our evolutionary journey into the unknown and the 21st century, with us embracing the Age of Aquarius, the golden age of potential and prosperity.

Manifestation is about being in the now, and being at one with you totally. We have to have clear intention when manifesting what we want, and to manifest it to the highest good of all. We must have no hidden agenda or purpose because if what we want is about our truth the manifestation would happen instantly.

CHAPTER 8

THE INFLUENCE OF PAST LIFETIMES

We have all been influenced by our past lifetimes at sometime or other, with some of us not being aware that we have. Our past lives play an important part in which we really are as they form parts of our characteristics and inherited traits. There will be a lot of people, who will not comfortable with the theory of us having past lives, this is purely each person's own choice, but it doesn't hurt for us to stay open minded because past lives can benefit us, if we allowed ourselves to be open to the bigger picture of our truth.

Every-one of us at times has experienced Déjà vu memories from long ago. We have all experienced the instant feeling of knowing someone that we've just met, having an infinite attraction. We have dreamed of places that we've never been too. In-fact we have had visions within our dreams and waking state, with memories being relived of some forgotten time. We have also experienced skills and talents that have come naturally to us, but also our vocations when suddenly we find a job that is second nature to us, offering us with contentment and fulfilment.

Past lives give us an in-sight into our true-selves, revealing hidden messages and the secrets to our present lifetime. These important in-sights allow us to gain the valuable information that would allow us to fully understand what our lives are all about. They help us to evolve with the continuance of the soul's quest, helping us to become whole and complete once more. The information about our past lives helps us to reinstate equilibrium within our everyday lives, allowing us to realign to the positive attributes of our past lives. Because within every past life that we address the more in-sight into our true-selves, and that of our true characters.

We have all come into this lifetime, to overcome important lessons that would set us free, from the restraints and restriction that we have found ourselves to be in. We all have problems within our lives, and we sometimes find ourselves making the same mistakes over and over again. Have you ever stopped to wonder why you keep attracting the same negative situations or circumstances? Thinking you had solved the problems within your life only to find that you'd not, leaving you wondering why and feeling discontent? When all we've been trying to do is overcome them to best of your ability.

We often find ourselves becoming frustrated or angry, because we didn't understand what it was all about, leaving us feeling perplexed. We then find that the negative undertones of our feelings have created an imbalance or disharmonious situation within. Which if left undetected would create the ailments, illness and eventually the diseases that we suffer from? Our past lives our about the imbalances that we have created for ourselves over the different centuries. We have allowed our emotional condemnations to affect our minds, and bodies, and more importantly our soul on the deeper fundamental levels of our Being.

We have all experienced past lives where only the negative traits are dealt with, maybe time running out before we could really enjoy the fruits of our labours. We would also have had very positive past lives where we successfully understood our lessons. Going on, to enjoy the positive aspects of those learning's activating our full potential, enabling us to achieve even greater things. Until that happens, we can only draw on the vibrations of those positive times in which to help us understand and overcome our problems within this lifetime.

So at first, my negativity had kept me in a place where I lived my life through the people I loved, all because I was in denial of my own life. Once I'd reconnected to the positive vibration of all lifetimes I then gave myself permission to pursue the reconnection of my truth, inner-self and higher consciousness. The realisation that I was worthy of putting my needs first, helped me to restore faith, belief and trust in myself. This granted me with the positive attributes of my higher self, a knowing that once I'd given to myself I was able to give to others successfully. There is a big difference between giving of you and giving up of you, something that we've all done at times.

When we achieve a balance within all aspects of our lives, will allow us more energy to help others but more importantly, we will know when to offer that help and support, so it's not at our detriment. When we are true to ourselves, helping others would become natural and instinctive, and more importantly pleasurable. This enables us to be really understanding of others and to be non-judgemental, only then being able to show love and compassion at all times.

When we experience love and joy in all that we do, say or think, makes our lives so rewarding, and allows us to have a life that just flows. This enables us to accomplish our dreams and desires effortlessly. When we do this, the universe can deliver it's abundance upon us, with us having a prosperous and healthy life. If we are not open to receiving or we think we don't deserve in some-way then the universe cannot deliver what we need or want. The way to know if you're open to receiving is when you are given a gift, can you accept it gracefully or are you embarrassed? If so, you're not open to receiving.

We are all a product of our own negative traits, everyone of us having pre-agreed to what would happen to us within any lifetime. We agreed to the different situations and circumstances of our lessons that we need to overcome, but whatever happens to us within this lifetime is about a configuration of numerous learning's, all part of the intricate learning's of our true destiny and of other lifetimes in order for us to become our true-selves once more.

When the time is right we choose when and how we overcome our problems, with us being mindful of the cause and effect of our actions, and to how they might affect the physical body or our minds, and even other individuals. To get an overall view of all situations we must look at the situations within our lives from others perspective as this gives us a deeper understanding of what's going on, because we then allow our peripheral vision to see a much bigger picture.

We all view life differently, so to see the bigger picture allows us to recognise the truth of any situation that we find us in which helps us to overcome then quickly. When we look at our past lives in the same way, we then get a better perspective of what this life is all about, and to how we can overcome our learning's in order to become our truth once more by activating our limitless potential from those lives. We also activate the infinite knowledge and wisdom, and like our conscious states that knowledge and wisdom also changes as we evolve and continue to learn.

In this lifetime I realised that the material trappings would not make me happy. We can put too much emphasis on the material trappings, thinking that the different things would make us feel better or happier about ourselves. We try to fill the voids within, instead of concentrating on what the voids are all about, and to what we have to do within our lives to elevate them. It's realising that we are important too and we need the consideration from us to achieve a well being state, instead of leaving things that needed attention until it's too late to sort them out. It's only when we lose someone dear to us or something that we cherished that we realise what's really important to us, missing it or them because they're no longer within our lives, and that goes for our health as well.

Our focus on material wealth makes us work harder to maintain the lifestyle that we've created for ourselves, believing that it makes our lives more rewarding. It's not the material wealth that's important but the people within our lives, and our relationship with them and us. So we owe it to us to become more self and body aware, which grants us with a long and healthy existence, whilst pursuing our dreams or goals.

When we experience hardship it creates a shift in our consciousness, and gives us the opportunity to show compassion and understanding of ourselves and others in order to overcome our life's experiences. There is nothing we can't overcome, but rather than being put to the test, let's get our values right as to what's really important within our lives, and that's us and our loved ones, because were irreplaceable.

Material wealth is lovely to have as long as our lives don't depend on it knowing it can be replaced, and demands so much of our time and money that at times it puts us under immense pressure. I had material wealth in this lifetime as well as other lifetimes, and it was the realisation it had not made me truly happy. At time I'd held on to the material wealth for security which created a false sense of happiness. At the time of our deaths the only thing that's important to us, is our loved ones that we're leaving behind, and that's what creates the most heartache for us in life, loosing those that we hold so dear.

When my first husband and I set off on our new life together, we would have lived in a shed as long as we were together. It's strange how our values in life changed; because we forgot to focus on the things that really mattered to us, all because we were working hard to maintain our lifestyle. My own unhappiness was created because I'd not allowed quality time for myself, consequently having an adverse affect on our relationship because we no longer had quality time together. This put far too much pressure on maintaining a balance, between motherhood, my relationship and work. By not recognising the imbalances within, I'd not realised how unhappy I was, until it was too late. We should have been more trusting of the other, and taken the time to care and nurture our relationship, and the life we shared together, instead of letting outside influences destroy what we'd achieved and worked so hard for.

With my life's purpose recognised and overcome, I am now the person I know I was always meant to be. I have embraced my power within, and reinstated a vibrational legacy that I can now take with me from lifetime to lifetime, the continuance of my soul's evolutionary journey. The lesson was, I did not deny myself, and I did what I was meant too, not just for me to learn from, but others too. My memories of all lifetimes live on within me and recorded in time within my collective consciousness; evolving with me just in case I need the information of those learning's to prevent me from making the same mistakes again whether in this life or future lifetimes.

Our soul's journey is to reconnect with the unique vibration of our higher consciousness and the creator, accessing our truth at all times. We must only have positive thoughts and our actions must be of the highest intention for all. We need to realise that what we give out, is what we get back. The reconnection of our full potential allows us to become a limitless being, manifesting all that we desire naturally. So we must be mindful of what we wish or crave for, because our thoughts are powerful, and what you wish for we can manifest good or bad.

So let me explain how the souls journey progresses by using some of my past lifetimes as an example; I had a lifetime back in 100,000BC in Atlantis, I was female and very privileged with great wealth. When I was 22 years old my parents chose a husband for me, and I married for status as apposed for love. I found this to be very hard as I didn't love my husband, and ended up resenting my life. I apparently had a good life but the underlining emotional imbalance was that I felt unfulfilled. I'd not realised that over a period of time I actually did fall in love with my husband but I hadn't acknowledged that fact whilst I was still alive. So I died feeling unfulfilled and not having experienced the true meaning of love!

I had another past lifetime in 47,000BC. I was blissfully happy and content, living the life that was intended with a husband and children by my side. I died naturally when the time came for me to return to the source. I had attained a high vibration, and was able to manifest all that I desired naturally, experiencing unconditional love on all levels, and in its truest form. Because in this lifetime I'd fully understood what love was all about!

My life's lessons were to understand all aspects of love, because we don't always appreciate the true meaning of love in the beginning of any relationship. It's the love we have at the end of our lifetime together that's true love. It is about the sharing and caring for each other, it's about experiencing and overcoming the good and bad times together, and it's being there for each other no matter what! We must all realise that we have a potential soul mate by our side, and that they too have similar life's lessons to learn and overcome. If we understand our problems together would allow us all to end our days with a soul-mate by our side.

The problems that we have within our relationship, requires the two of them to sort it out, with us not feeling threatened or insecure by the decisions that the other makes. This applies to all relationships that we have, and we must all work hard at maintaining equilibrium, and sharing wonderful times together because all relationships are to be valued.

The most important learning that I experienced was the importance of self love because if we do not love ourselves, others cannot love us successfully. If we do not love us, we have nothing to measure love by. When we do not love ourselves we lose faith, belief, and trust in us and others. Self-love is our power to ignite our truth and limitless potential, and then we live our lives surrounded by unconditional love.

Our soul's journey and quest is about us integrating with every positive aspect of us, and that includes our past incarnate lives that are relevant to our ascension. We have all been on our soul's journey through the different centuries, gathering the infinite knowledge and wisdom that would allow us to become our collective consciousness since time began. It is important to our ascended soul to integrate with every aspect of us which makes us whole and complete, and powerful once more.

This is our soul's true quest; for all is encompassing and all things come back into one, we have to learn how to be ascended but in human form, and this will allow our vibration to play its role in the purification and cleansing process of humankind. Once this has been achieved others will reconnect to their authentic self in readiness of the enlightened journey that awaits them also.

Through the different centuries we have all experienced great changes especially within our vibrations, and as we allow our vibrations to change yet again, we will evolve to a higher vibrational human being. The Age of Aquarius is about the purification and cleansing of the earth's structure and all human being, with us all going through a transition of great growth, personally and spiritually. With this new age comes new beginning for us all of great wealth, happiness and exposure to our limitless potential of all lifetimes. When we integrate with every aspect of us, and with everyone we've ever been since time began, we can accomplish our potential effortlessly.

Life is what we make it so let's embrace this evolutionary age because we've all waited a very long time to participate and achieve our higher consciousness status once again which aids us on our pathway to freedom and ascension.

CHAPTER 9

EMBRACE THE POWER WITHIN

Embracing the power within is to embrace our high conscious self in its truest form. Over many lifetimes and even throughout this lifetime we will at sometime or other have disconnected from our higher conscious self, with us all having being connected at our birth. The disconnection of our higher conscious self happens because we've stopped believing in us or we don't trust or have faith in us anymore. There are numerous reasons as to why this disconnection from our higher self happens; but it leaves us struggling with our everyday lives, with us having to work harder to achieve our dreams or goals. We should be all doing less in order to achieve more, and not doing more to achieve less, as we all seem to do at sometime or other!

When we're ready, and after we've experienced a journey of self discovery and awareness, we will find ourselves fully understanding our negative issues or blocks. When we alleviate these imbalances or the unrest from within the mind, body or soul, we then achieve the ultimate connection of the higher conscious self. The secret to successfully alleviating negative imbalances, illness and disease is to be totally committed to seeking well being state, on all levels of existence. We must be dedicated to achieving wholeness and completion to our mind, body and soul. We do this in order to be healthy, and to fulfil our dreams or goals achieving a prosperous life. When we release all negative imbalances on a higher conscious level, we reconnect to the collective consciousness of humankind, our creator, and truth which is our infinite power within.

So what is our power within? It's our reconnection to our unique gifts, skills, and abilities that ignite the power of our higher consciousness, and the infinite knowledge and wisdom that we've attained over all lifetimes. There are many pathways available to us to help us achieve this reconnection, but first we need to rediscover our authentic self by becoming self and body aware of all the different aspects of us, in order to restore health on every level of our existence.

Essential Self; we need to reconnect with our essential self, the essence of our angelic presence. Our essential self is who we really are from when time began, and in times of anguish, trauma or hardship we could lose touch or disconnect from our essential self in order to protect us, maybe hiding us deep within. We can at times of great trauma project our essential self in an outwardly direction putting us somewhere safe until we have recovered from whatever is going on within our lives. I once met a lady who had projected her essential self into a beloved horse, the horse had given her comfort and love at a time when she was being sexually abused! Someone else had buried their essential self deep within them, thinking they were not worthy and consequently had no self esteem or love. So! It's important that we own our Essential self as it's the purity of our soul.

Inner Being; we need to reconnect to our inner being; our being is who we really are within this lifetime and we should own our inner being 100%. When we strive to be liked or loved we give up of ourselves, we do this in order to be accepted or to seek approval. This happens at times when we experience self doubt or feelings of insecurity, not realising that by self doubting we give our power away. We normally give up of ourselves to others or a cause! This makes them more powerful than us, and depending on the percentage that we've give away, depends on what we get back for our efforts. For example say we had give 47% of us away to someone else or a cause in order to feel good about us or to survive our everyday lives. Whatever we tried to achieve we would give 100% of us, thinking it was our best efforts; the reward for our efforts would only be 53%. This leaves us feeling that life's not fair, because the efforts outweigh the rewards. At times this can leave us feeling very despondent, and then we risk becoming disheartened with us believing all our efforts will end in failure.

Intuition; we need to rediscover our intuitiveness, and trust in our gut reactions. Throughout our lives some of us lose touch with our intuition not trusting or acting on that small voice or thought within. If we let this happen we struggle through life, and our life's lessons or purpose becomes hard work for us to understand or even learn from. So it's important that we trust our intuition and gut reactions 100% in order to access the hidden messages that come from our higher conscious self and soul, they speak gently to us, telling us what we need to know and at times what to do. So to trust in our Intuition is life changing, and enhances our life when we listen to those instinctive feelings or thoughts of our intuition guiding us forwards.

Self Love; you will be amazed how many people do not like or even love themselves. We need to love us in order to reconnect to the power within, self love is very important to restoring health on every level of our being. A lack of self-love makes us think we do not deserve in some way, and so we think we are not important enough to want health, wealth and happiness. We fall out of love with ourselves for lots of different reasons, maybe thinking we're being punished because our lives are not how we want or envisaged them to be. Our negative feelings stop us from achieving all that we desire, so we become frustrated with us and our lives, and risk falling out of love with us. We then make others the focus of our love by giving and giving, all because we do not love ourselves enough to say no to the demands of others. On a scale of 1 to 10 how much do you love yourself, with 10 being you do? To reinstate Self Love is priceless, and you do this by being kind and considerate to you, treating yourself as you would your best friend.

Self Belief: is believing in yourself no matter what! We might not recognise that we don't always believe in us, all because life's problems can take its toll on us which leaves us struggling with our day to day lives. We sometimes find ourselves having belief in things outside of us and others, and have no belief in us in- order to achieve what we want or need. When we reinstate self belief we no longer look to others to provide or achieve things for us, and we then start living our lives for ourselves in earnest, because when we have faith in us, so do others.

Self Faith: to have self faith is to know yourself completely, and to have faith in every aspect of you. We have to have faith in God, faith in others to do the right thing, faith that what we hoped for will come into fruition. More importantly to have faith in ourselves, our intuitive self, and knowing self, in order to fulfil our dreams and ambitions to the highest good of all. To reinstate self faith is to honour us, and all our accomplishments.

Self Trust: to have self trust is to honour and respect every aspect of you and to know you are an honourable person. When we trust us we can make the right decisions in our truth, and with no hidden agenda. We must trust ourselves to have rightful intention, but also to trust that everything we need will be provided for. To reinstate self trust is to have conviction and courage in us, and in all we achieve truthfully.

Heal our Heart; to heal our heart or broken heart is very important to our well being. Throughout our lives and because of life's experiences we lose heart or we take the negative emotions to heart, which creates negative imbalances within the heart. Some of us are no longer open hearted because of a need to survive and protect us, and it's too painful to risk our heart being damaged or broken again! We need to acknowledge that our hearts need nurturing, which allows us to release the hurts or any other disharmonious emotions in order for us to heal our hearts, and become open hearted once again enabling us to receive all that we need positively.

After my divorce I felt my heart had been broken into a million pieces, for years I was afraid to become open hearted again. So I protected myself and within my heart I held hurt, betrayal, rejection and disillusionment. It's only after healing our broken heart that we realise the importance of healing our Heart in order to feel whole once more.

Heal our Soul; to heal our soul is important to our soul's journey and the journey of evolution. Within any lifetime we end up giving fragmentations of our souls away to the people we love, sometimes just to be accepted or liked, even to the point of selling a proportion of our souls for what we believe is right. By trying too hard to please or gain respect from others we risk giving too much of us away, to the point that we then make others more important than us. We can also leave soul fragmentations of us in different countries or places especially if we did not have a say to what happened to us, by others making choices for us. It is important that our soul is healed, and made whole once more in order to retain our power of divinity. Not only do we give fragmentations of our soul to others, we can also have fragmentations of other peoples, so all fragmentations of the soul has to be returned to their rightful owners in order for them to heal, and for us all to heal our soul completely.

Heal Baby in the Womb; it is important to heal us as a baby in the womb, because even from conception we take on negative emotions from those around us. We can be affected by anguish and trauma that may have affected our parents during the pregnancy. To heal the baby in the womb gives us our right and place to be within this lifetime, and also to feel whole, protected and loved. When healing us in the womb gives us the overwhelming feeling of unconditional love throughout our lives, and connects us to the purity and truth of a child.

Inner Child; to heal our inner child brings laughter and joyfulness back into our lives. It is important to reconnect with the innocence of our inner child but also the freedom it gives us because when we trust our true-selves, it helps alleviate anguish and trauma or even fears that are held within. Healing our inner child brings wholeness to our inner and true self, and allows us to trust our instincts once more. The more we nurture our inner child the more we grow, and evolve to the higher conscious levels, eagerly enjoying our lives once again, connected to our Inner Child and in truth, with love and joy within our lives.

The methods I used were the art of Kinesiology, and more recently Theta Healing but also I had an intensive understanding of most alternative remedies or holistic therapies. Natural healing happens when you understand why you have a medical problem in the first place. Sometimes we just have the symptoms, but if ignored become a condition, then an illness or disease. So with the unique understanding as to why you have a medical problem or maybe you just feel blocked and need to sort your problems out, which helps us to restore health by being body aware.

Convention medicines and alternative approaches go hand in hand when healing the mind, body and soul, when we reinstate the unique gifts of our authentic self, we become self and body aware in order to improve our health and life. When we connect with the collective consciousness of us, we can heal our life, but also our vibrations allow others to heal their lives as long as they are committed to doing so.

I choose a self discovery approach to going within to understand what was going on around or within me, and the more self and body aware I became, the more understanding I had of what was going on, and to what I'd done to me! It's by asking yourself a simple question like why do I feel angry? But you must allow yourself to be truthful with your answer. Maybe your angry was because you'd let yourself down by not fulfilling a promise or the task that you'd set yourself was at times unrealistic, and you'd put yourself under too much pressure with the challenges of life, and then becoming too stressful. I have seen great phenomena of people addressing illness or disease, only to make a complete recovery once they have been truthful with themselves as why they had the condition in the first place.

So by sitting quietly and going within allows us to feel the unrest of our souls. We need to hypothetically scan the inside of us, with our inner senses or vision by going within any area of the mind or body that feels out of balance. We need to expose the area within us where we'd stored the negativity that's been caused by an emotional anguish or trauma, that over a period of time could have manifested into some disharmonious condition. Once we understand the imbalance or condition we can then release whatever the imbalance was, in order to achieve well being.

When we release the imbalance we have a more positive approach to life, and a new thought process that allows us to perceive the truth of all things naturally. This process allows us to know why things happen to us, in order to never repeat the same olds thought patterns or negative perception of thinking we are being punished in some-way or we've made a wrong decision. Acceptance of all things good or bad will allow us to stay healthy of mind, body or soul by naturally releasing all that does not serve our higher self anymore.

We have to empower every aspect of us in order to change the different things within, and with our lives. Any self work we do on us is life changing, but it also gives us compassion and understanding of not only ourselves but other too. Once we've reinstated the essential elements listed above we'll begin to feel whole but not complete. In order to feel complete we must reconnect with our higher conscious self, the divine and universal energy of our creator. So with our feet firmly on the floor, and our minds energy reaching upwards will connect us to our higher conscious self, the divine, and universal energy, that reinstates our connection with the ultimate vibration of the collective consciousness of humankind, this is our unique power!

CHAPTER 10

EMPOWERED AFFIRMATIONS

When we embrace the power within we are consciously making a commitment to us, to empower or re-educate us into positive action or thinking. When we embrace our infinite power we can change the way we think which promotes focus and intention whilst achieving our goals.

I have designed a technique that is easy and effective to use with us feeling more positive straight away, and I've published as a self help book, it's called (The Empowered Affirmations Balancing Technique).

Once we have a clear vision of what we want to achieve we can empower us to achieve it. With focus and intention we can rebalance our energy field within and around the physical body, having a positive effect on our minds which then influences and empowers every aspect of our lives. We start to attract all that we need in a positive and successful way, allowing us to take back the control of our lives, and true destiny. We have to embrace the infinite power of us that's located within our hearts, so by placing our hand over the heart we're already making a commitment to us to change our life, and by altering our thought process or pattern we can make positive changes.

The balancing technique I've designed is just one way of empowering yourself, and will leave you feeling empowered by your own infinite energy, with atonement and realignment of the mind, body and soul straight away. When we place our hand over the heart it helps us to focus on reprogramming or reinforcing the promises that we are now making to us. Empowered affirmations have a profound effect on the mind that influences the body and empowers our soul. This process allows old programming, thought patterns and negative belief's to dissolve, by altering our states of awareness and perceptions. Any positive affirmation or command has an adverse effect on how the mind responds, and then influences the physical body which alters our states of consciousness.

The more evolved we are the less our physical bodies are effected by our negative emotions or outside influences which allows us to achieve a well being state. This lifetime is about us all having a heavenly life in a human form, and not the one we've created for us out of our unhappiness. Our life's journey is to reconnect with our personal power within accessed at a higher conscious level, this is our soul's mission because once we've embraced our higher conscious self we can manifest our dreams successfully.

The main affirmation I use is; *I am my infinite power* because that is our truth!

I have listed below some of our negative beliefs or illusions that we quite often experience in order for us to feel good about us but then we often have to justify our actions or thoughts.

1.   We can often give up of ourselves to help others, when in-fact our needs are greater, maybe focusing on them means we do not have to focus on us.

2.   We project our love onto others at a time when we don't love or even like us anymore, maybe feeling unloved.

3.   We say we are alright when in-fact we are not.

4.   We get angry with others when in-fact we are angry at ourselves, and don't know why?

5.   We feel we are being punished in some-way, when we are punishing the self. Often beating us up over things we thought we had got wrong or for not achieving our dreams, when we'd made a promise to us to do so.

70

6. We say we are not bothered by some situation or other, when in-fact we are!

7. We say yes to things when we mean no! Maybe not loving ourselves enough to say no to the demands of others.

8. We deny ourselves of things because we think we are not worthy or deserving in some-way.

9. We self-doubt, then end up giving our power away to someone else, thinking they know better.

10. We project our insecurities onto others, which then allow us to feel secure.

11. We put restrictions within our life, when we are fearful about moving forwards.

12. We stop believing in us because we have lost inner faith, belief, and trust, in us and life.

13. We feel threaten by the choices or decisions made by others, because we are afraid to make our own.

14. We feel lonely and depressed because we no longer take responsibility for us.

15. We are never betrayed unless we have betrayed ourselves first, by not living the life that was intended, instead of the one created from our insecurities.

16. We often experience a lack of trust, faith, belief, and love for ourselves, which causes us to disconnect from our higher conscious self, and the infinite energy of the creator, and that of our truth.

17. Procrastination of the self, will eventually lead to blaming others for the things that our wrong within our lives. With us thinking that we did not have a choice, to what's happening to us so just went along with it!

18.   Procrastination can also lead to fall out of love with God, the Self or Others.

19.   Our negative emotions are positive emotions as long as we acknowledge them, and take action to alleviate them.

20.   When we are not fully in our lives we just go through the process of living in the past or the future, but not in the present time! With us wasting our time until things get better but taking a huge risk that they never will, until we take positive action, and change our mindsets of how we perceive the different situations or circumstances within our lives.

When we reinstate equilibrium between the mind, body and soul, we reconnect with the universal life-force energy that sustains all growth, whether it's physically, mentally, emotionally or spiritually. This guarantees us with continued success in all areas of our lives, allowing us to achieve our dreams, goals and visions. So once we recognise the imbalances within, we can introduce a new thought process that allows us to become positive in the decisions we then make. We need to recognise, and seize the opportunities as they present themselves to us, knowing with confidence that they are the small steps we need to take, in order to realise, and reach our limitless potential. We need to accept that we're already living part of our dreams or ambitions, and this process will allow us to be living our lives successfully in the Now!

So depending on your emotional, physical, mental or spiritual issues will denotes what sort of affirmation would be most beneficial for you. An empowered affirmation is a promise your making to you, so write a promise or a statement of your own onto a piece of paper in order to empower you when reciting it, because any empowered affirmation is a positive statement or command that empowers you into positive thinking and action, with courage, conviction and confidence.

I list a few of my affirmations in order for you to see the effect they can have on you if recited:

I trust in my life's experiences and I love myself unconditionally.

I have clear conviction of my truth and I trust in my higher conscious self.

I release my negative thoughts and feelings and it's safe to be my truth now.

I release all that's no longer relevant to my life's purpose or lessons.

I am at peace and comfortable with every stage of my life.

My life is in perfect balance and harmony and I move forwards in my life with ease and confidence.

I go beyond my fears and limitations and create the life I want.

I open my heart and only create loving relationships, I am love and I attract love now.

I choose this life for its experiences and lessons in order to set myself free to become my truth.

My inner being loves it's self.

I have self love and I release my fears now.

I have self faith, trust and belief in me and I release my fears now.

I give myself permission to move forwards in my life easily and effortlessly.

I forgive myself and all situations.

I give myself permission to be the best I can be.

I attract the power of money and release the fears of my debts now.

It is with love that I totally release the past.

My higher conscious self is my intuitive knowing.

I create a life filled with joy and laughter.

My life is full of abundance and I am wealthy.

I release all restraints and restrictions within my life and I am free to be me.

I relax and go with the flow of life and all that I need comes to me.

I choose this life for its experiences and lessons, and to become my limitless potential now.

My life is rich with love and joy and I embrace all that life has bestowed upon me.

I love my life and life loves me, and I am free to be the best I can be.

I lovingly take care and nourish my mind, body and soul.

I empower myself to be successful in all I do, and I will succeed and bring my dreams into fruition.

I empower myself to be my higher conscious self and truth at all times.

These are just a few ideas of affirmations that you can empower yourself with or compose an affirmation that is more appropriate to what's going on within your life, and will allow you to rebalance your energy to be more positive. This process will give you courage and conviction to move forwards with your life and make positive decision.

If you would like to try the balancing technique it's performed whilst standing upright with your feet apart for balance. Connect with mother earth with your feet to give you stability and a firm foundation on which to build the rest of your life upon. Then allow your minds energy to connect with your higher consciousness and universal energies. Then place your hand over the heart as this automatically connects you to the thymus, one of the main organs within the body that is affected through stress, and the second is the heart because we take things to heart if we feel we've failed in some-way or we've put ourselves under too much pressure.

So once you've decided on your empowered affirmation recite in a clear decisive manner. Close your eyes, take a deep breath in, hold and connect with your higher consciousness and universal energy, as you breathe out, say out loud I am my infinite power and then allow your mind, body, and soul to rebalance.

When you experience the balancing technique your body will rock or sway backwards and forwards, and only when you stabilise or have the erg to plunge forwards are you balanced. The swaying sensation can be a gentle, where as the rocking sensation can be a forceful as this normally denotes the extent of the imbalance within. If you've only swayed gently it's

75

because you were slightly out of balance instead of being totally out of balance if you rocked back and forth.

You can rebalance your body's energy of the imbalances or disharmonious situations that's within anytime you like, as you're just empowering you to be more positive which can only enhance lives. The more body aware you become the higher your consciousness will be, and in this state of consciousness you can make commands to have your burdens, ailments, illness or diseases removed from within your mind, body or soul naturally and effortlessly.

We can also address our feelings, negative beliefs or programs that are held within our mind, body or soul just the same by making simple commands to empower the self. Because we then alter our conscious mindset by replacing any negative thought with positive affirmations that re-programs or re-educate us to become our higher conscious self at all times. We can then perform healing or miracles, with us naturally using our unique gifts, skills and abilities to the highest good of all, and becoming our limitless potential of all lifetimes!

All because you've Embraced the Power Within.

CHAPTER 11

ENLIGHTENED TO THE FUTURE

When we have become enlightened we can face our future with confidence and conviction, and our futures hold huge potential as we become the person that we use to be, but centuries ago. Once we have become our higher conscious self, and successfully access all that we need, we will be living our lives in truth with us manifesting all that we desire naturally.

Enlightenment means to be enlightened to our true self, the truth and our ability to predict the future for us. We can't predict what might happen in the future as we have no control over the different situations, but we can predict what we want to happen for us. We must have pure intention and conviction, when projecting what we want to achieve or accomplish but in an enlightened state, we would then be naturally accepting of all situations, and wait patiently for them to materialize.

Each individual can change themselves in order to create a positive future for them and others, but only when we're clear and realistic in the goals that we set ourselves. We can influence the present and the future, but we can't influence the past, we all have to accept what's passed. It's important to be in the now because this is where we experience everything and everyone, and interaction with all aspects of our lives will allow us all to prepare for our future. To be enlightened to our future is to know what we want from our lives, which allow us to relive our dreams, and accomplishments that were very rewarding and fulfilling in other centuries. To manifest want we want, we need to be in the now and within our power, in order to manifest correctly and successfully.

Thousands of people are quietly awakening to their higher consciousness, and thousands more have already been awakened. Although people may derive inspiration, moral codes, and even wisdom from the religious texts, and great authors of spiritual matters, it's all a second hand experience. When we're awakened to our enlightened-self we'll experience inspiration and wisdom first hand, and our own moral codes is intuitive and pure, because we can do no more than to act with integrity in all that we do.

We can't prepare for the unknown, we can only prepare ourselves for what we want to be or do. Spirituality has come a full circle because in the past we needed these learning's or teachings in order to open us up to the higher vibrations of our enlightened self. We are now in an age where these changes are spontaneous, with us all going through the evolutionary age of the activation of our higher consciousness. Our higher conscious vibration is the evolutionary energy of the Kundalini which promotes the spiritual awakening of human kind.

The more that everyone understands what's happening to them with the empowerment of this tremendous life force energy of the kundalini, and to understand the implications to individuals and our planet, the more easily and quickly we'll all reap the benefits. The energy of the kundalini resides within us all, and over the centuries we've been waiting for this incredible energy to be reactivated. Over the last twenty years or so, people have been actively trying to raise their kundalini energy that's lay dormant in a reservoir at the base of our spine. The vibration of our earth as changed in order for this evolutionary energy of the kundalini to be spontaneously released once again, as we all go through purification and cleansing process, but not just us but our world also. The kundalini is the reawakening of the collective consciousness of humankind.

Our world is going through the same cleansing process as each individual, and it's about our mass-negativity being exposed in order for life changing action to be made in order to overcome this important process and with us all taking part in eradicating the worlds mass-negativity. Each individual who is raising their kundalini will be made aware of the things within their lives and selves that needs attention, and with consideration will promote positive action in achieving a well being state. Once we have achieved our purpose, we will take an active role in the guidance of others to do the same.

Too much of today's counselling is for the effect and not the cause of our ailments, illness or disease. Improper energy flow within us all is the main cause of many emotional and mental problems; it's about us not getting caught up in the emotional and mental conflict of the self. We make life so complicated for us, because of our ignorance of this life force energy of the universe, and to how we have allowed our physical bodies to become depleted from this unique energy that would have promoted self-healing of our mind, body and soul naturally.

To be enlightened for our future is a big wake up call for us all, and we owe to us to take an active role in securing a positive future for us and others. The secret to life is to allow this change to happen naturally, by clearing our sub-conscious and conscious minds of all negativity. We have all completed a cyclic age in evolution, because spirituality is to be spirit conscious which makes us aware of everything and everyone. Spirit conscious is to be aware of all things, past, present and for us to be prepared to create a positive future. Healing our sub-conscious and conscious minds will naturally release ailments, illness and disease, but first we must actively seek the understanding of how we survive within the structure of our world.

The life force energy is encouraging growth emotionally, physically, mentally and spiritually, with the development of our brains in order to accommodate this evolutionary energy of the universe. Parts of our brains have been dormant for centuries but are now slowly being reawakened to support the infinite knowledge and wisdom that sustains all growth, and it's important to us in overcoming all of life's lessons. We need to do less within our lives in order to achieve more, and by having the foresight and pure intension when in pursuit of our dreams or goals. We make life hard work for us at times, and we block us because of our insecurities or emotional turmoil. To go with the flow of life, allows the different aspects of life to come to us, by being our higher conscious and powerful self. We are then connected to our collective consciousness and universal energies, achieving abundance in all we do.

Our earth is naturally going through its own purification and cleansing process, slowing taking back what's being taken and miss-used over many centuries but a lot of people are feeling the effects, and they are not even sure they'll survive. We can't argue with the life force energy of nature, and it cannot be controlled, it has to be respected because it naturally finds its own way back to its original origin or essence. The same applies to us, for we too are trying to find our way back to our original form, but in the meantime we have to go with the flow of life in order to life abundantly within our chosen lifestyles.

Once we become our higher consciousness we can manifest a positive future for all, without the need to destroy our planet and the people upon it. We have to live in harmony and peace with unity between all things, and we do this by being to true to us, and honouring our promise that we made a long time ago. The promise was to release our life's burdens and surrender to the will of heaven, by being our higher conscious self. We then become enlightened to what we've done to us, has we've suppressed our negative emotions which at times made us feel ill or hard done too. Whatever's happened to us we've allowed to happen but a very long time ago, hence our life's purpose to undo what we perceived wrongly, centuries ago.

In order to walk the pathway to a successful future, all we need to do is think with our higher conscious mind, and not our lower conscious mind, and those who've already reconnected with their higher conscious mind, need to think with their ascended mind. A higher conscious person would be someone aware of the negativity within and around them, but have chosen a pathway of self-discovery and awareness, to better themselves on all levels of existence.

An ascended person would have sorted their problems out long ago, and they are no longer affected by the emotional and mental problems but walk purposefully along their chosen pathway oblivious of the mass-negativity. They would only see the good in everyone and everything, and their evolutionary energy would radiate outwards to naturally purify and cleanse everything within the structure of our world. They would guide the human race into The Golden Age of Aquarius where we can all achieve our limitless potential in order to secure a better future for us all. This is the mission of humankind, and eventually we'll all take this evolutionary journey when we're ready to do so.

We have a very unsettled time in front of us all has we embrace this new age, there will be lots of disruption as the earth continues to go through its purifying and cleansing process. It does not have to be all doom and gloom because we can rise above the disasters by focusing on us in preparation for a positive future. If we allow our vibrations to rise above the negativity we can focus us on us becoming enlightened in order to get our lives back on track.

Unfortunately we all have to ride the storms of our own doing for a few more years, but the more people that's raise their vibrations will make a huge difference to us and our planet. So the more we can recruit into taking this evolutionary journey the quicker we'll all get there. This is a vibrational world that we live in, and it responds to whatever vibrations we send out, negatively or positively. It is a vicious circle, so we must make positive changes for the better because what we give out is then what we'll get back!

Beyond 2023 we'll see a great change in our climate for the better, and we'll see a positive change in our nation as a whole. We'll be less demanding on our resources with technology being able to achieve more with less affect on our world's resources, with the invention of incredible energy saving devises and equipment. The change is already happening with the internet taking over from us being busy fools, of running around when we can achieve things far more easily, with just a touch of a button. The internet connects souls worldwide, in order to access consciously what we need in pursuit of our dreams or goals. This gives us more family time if used correctly, but again this is something that has to be achieved consciously by weighing up the pros and cons.

Everything happens for a reason and sometimes we're at a loss to know what that reason is? So we must be accepting and embrace things that we have no control over, knowing somewhere deep within us is the solution to all of our problems. Deep within us is all is the desire and urgency to overcome the transition of us and our world into this new age of great potential. We've been through the different stages of evolution before but not in this incarnate form but others. We have survived and then died, and then chosen another lifetime, because we've all been waiting for this moment in time! We all know deep within us what we have to do in order to survive the transformation of our world, but to do it consciously attuned to our higher consciousness and true-selves, and the collective consciousness of all.

We are over populated at present with lots of souls walking our earth plane, whether physically or spiritually but that's because all souls are taking part in the transformation of this evolutionary age of our soul's quest and the continuance of a journey into unknown territory. We will all at sometime or other in the future, evolve to other dimensions within the solar system of our universe. So let's put our best foot forwards has our futures positively await us!

CHAPTER 12

OUR LIMITLESS POTENTIAL

Our limitless potential is the positive attributes of us and of all lifetimes that we have incarnated in, and they are our greatest achievements of all times. Our life's mission is to evolve the realms of our lower conscious lives by letting go of the restraints and restrictions, and our negative beliefs or programming that we've held ourselves too. We have to transcend the limitations of the material world, evolving to a higher conscious perspective of what life is all about, and to what's really important within our lives. When we live our lives as a higher consciousness being allows our vibrations to alter and change frequency in order to become more in-tune with the universe and earths energies. The more refined our vibrations become, the more attuned we are to every aspect of our world and us, which inspires us to become our limitless potential of all lifetimes.

Our mission for this lifetime is to overcome and understand our life's purpose, all being part of our karmic debt to others in order to go onto achieve our limitless potential of all lifetimes but within this lifetime. When we understand why we're here in this incarnate existence, we can let go of any past life trauma, imbalance or negative beliefs or programming. We can heal our past lives as well as this one, and achieve health, wealth, and happiness in all that we do once again. This will set us free to evolve to a higher vibrational level or plane, in order to live the prosperous life that was intended for us so long ago.

We choose to be born into this century because we didn't want to miss out on the opportunity of realising what our limitless potential was all about. Over the centuries we have experienced many incarnate lives, and some of those lives are relevant to this lifetime, because the memories of which are stored with the blueprint of our collective memory. Those memories are about our gifts, skills or abilities and unique talents that we'd achieved or experienced and they're important to helping us become our truth once more. They influence our lives in order for us to reconnect with their ultimate vibration so we can achieve things beyond our wildest dreams. Our limitless potential will have us achieving and accomplishing anything that we set our minds too, and with a positive mindset, clear conviction and focus, allows us to manifest what we want effortlessly.

Each and everyone of us at sometime or other will go through a series of initiations of integrating with the different aspects of us from other lifetimes as well as this one, in order to become whole and complete. We do this with the intention of becoming our infinite power, because each aspect or fragmentation of us has been influencing our lives for a very long time. When we do not recognise that fact, leaves us giving our power away by thinking someone else other than us is providing what we need or want. The reasons behind what we need or want can be influenced by our emotional insecurities which denote if we can manifest them. When we are our infinite power, we can manifest our needs or wants almost instantly, with the power of our thoughts playing a part with intention and conviction.

Our limitless potential is to recognise all that we've achieved, accomplish or done since time began, and it's ours to tap into once we've understood how the collective consciousness of us works. We are our higher conscious self, and we're on an ascended path with us all eventually becoming our ascended self, empowering us to be successful in every aspect of our lives.

We are the power of our limitless potential, higher consciousness and ascended self, and we need to embrace that power. The reason why we've not embraced the power within us is because we thought the power was outside of us, when it's not. We have all been waiting for the much needed wakeup call to the fact it's within, because we've hypothetically travelled the universe and back again, in search of what we felt was missing from within our lives that would enlighten us. What we've been searching for was already within us, just waiting for us to reconnect with once more, and it's called our limitless potential of our collective vibration of which we've ever been since time began!

We can connect with our limitless potential by allowing our minds energy to expand upwards, and we do this by reaching upwards connecting to our higher conscious self. We then empower us by connecting with our twin self who was hypothetically an artist in a past lifetime, and we allow the vibration of that lifetime as an artist to inspire us. We need to see us in our minds eye creating a masterpiece, we then sense the mood of the artist and feel their inspiration. Then we visualise us painting our masterpiece, and allow our-self to see the picture hanging in an art gallery and then being sold. When satisfied that you've inspired and empowered yourself, you can then create your own masterpiece in the present sense. But remember we all need to start somewhere, and you'll be amazed how quickly you learn if you let yourself be inspired by your twin self. Just allow yourself to blend with the positive attributes of you from another lifetime, centuries ago.

We can inspire us to be anything we want, and with a positive mindset we can achieve things beyond our wildest dreams. Years ago I use to play golf with a group of men, but because I was not a serious player I use to ask my higher conscious self to allow the best of the best golf player, to play through me or with me, and at times when I allowed myself to totally blend with that aspect of me I would take a fantastic shot, which often left the others amazed at how I'd achieved a shot that they'd messed up or miss calculated. This was a technique I used years ago, and at the time I didn't really understand what I was doing because I did it instinctively. I now know I was empowering me with a potential successful me from another lifetime who was an incredible golf player.

This technique can be used to empower yourself to be anything you want, because over the centuries we have been successful people as we've experienced all vocations, past times or hobbies, and we have a wealth of knowledge and experience. We have all achieved great things that have given us satisfaction and wealth, and we have an infinite range of knowledge and wisdom at our disposal. All we need to do is just empower us to be the best we can be, really it's just mind over matter.

For those who have experienced a spiritual journey of communicating with spirit guides, and ascended masters or even the angelic realms have been communicating with different aspects of themselves from long ago. So when we ask a spirit guide, angel or even an ascended master to work with us, we are basically or hypothetically talking to our higher conscious or ascended us to do this, that or the other for us. We are asking an aspect of us to achieve what we want for us, we're empowering an aspect of us to manifest what we want.

The same theory applies when we ask God, we're hypothetically asking the God part of us to perform a miracle or deed, and by not been aware of this we fall into the illusion that someone else is providing or performing the miracle or deed. When in fact it's us that's sent the vibrational thought out into the universe, and then we have to see if we have what it takes to bring or manifest what we want into our lives consciously. So when we don't get what we've asked for, it's us that's let us down because it's about intention, and self effort to manifest our desires or dreams for us, but consciously.

Our limitless potential is every aspect of us from all lifetimes since time began, and we need to reconnect with that potential because that's our infinite power within. When we recognise that fact, we can then become our truth and definitive power, and have the life that was intended for us long ago but more importantly to be living our lives to the best of our abilities, and the potential is huge.

CHAPTER 13

SOUL'S MISSION

The soul's mission is to evolve, and eventually transform back to its original form, from when time began in preparation for the next evolutionary stage of existence. The soul as evolved over many centuries going through all the different levels of existence in order to experience all aspects of life, and too see if we could achieve a life living in truth and connected to our definitive power.

Through the different incarnate lives the soul as encountered and accumulated mass negativity through the miss-understanding of the soul's true mission. This negativity can be on a small scale or a huge scale but it still has to be dealt with. Our negativity is accumulated in many ways from emotional, spiritual, physical and mental imbalances of what we perceived wrongly. Over the centuries each person's negative imbalances had caused them to disconnect from their higher conscious and ascended self that would have naturally alleviated any negativity before their deaths. Instead of us having to come back into another lifetime to try and sort our problems out.

Through each incarnate life the soul would have experienced the different stages of existence, with us being highly evolved in some lives, and disconnected from the higher conscious of humankind in others. All brought on by what we're exposed to or to what we've experienced in order to learn from, and hopefully to reconnect with the power or the essence of our original form before we departed the earth plane. Through the different stages of evolution, souls have become detached from their collective consciousness whilst living on the earth plane, and only reconnect with it once they've returned to the source of their origin, hypothetically heaven as we know it.

My belief is that after every incarnate life, we take the negativity with us that we've accumulated whilst on the earth plane, with the intention of understanding why we've allowed the negative aspects of our lives to affect us they way that we had. We all should have dealt with our negative issues correctly whilst on earth, instead of taking it with us upon our deaths. This is why we come back into another life to try, and rectify our miss-understandings. Our life's purpose is about understanding the negative aspects of us, and then eradicating the imbalance we've created within the structure of our world. Every action, thought or deed is a living vibration that evolves with us all from lifetime to lifetime, and this is one of the reasons that the earth's vibration as been affected by the world's mass negativity and it has to be eradicated.

I have experienced and understood through past life regression some of my past lifetimes, and to what the overall purpose of my soul was all about. So I will explain my life back in the late eighteen hundreds in order for you to understand the importance of our soul's mission and quest. My name was Mary Jane Kelly and I was a victim of the notorious Jack the Ripper in 1888. I was murdered in the most gruesome way which caused my soul to be earthbound and traumatised for a very long time. I was eventually re-born into this century in 1953, and after past life regression and a journey of healing Mary's soul, she was finally released from her dreadful ordeal, and was laid to rest.

The journey I encountered was informative, and mind blowing at times, has other victims of Jack where also re-born into this century in order for the mass negativity of Jack the Ripper to be dealt with. Once I'd learnt of my past-life history, people started to make themselves known to me who was also incarnated within that same century. First was PC James Harvey who was a policeman at the time of those dreadful murders, he had a friendship with Mary, and was devastated by her murder. For those who have read my book about Jack and Mary will know that PC James Harvey was the reincarnation of my twin flame Gary who I'd met within this lifetime in order to write the story of Jack and Mary and to deal with their torment.

The next was a dear friend who'd been in my life for years and I always felt infinity with her, but didn't know the connection until I was writing the book. What transpired was she was the reincarnation of one of the other victims, in fact over a period of twelve months the entire victim's reincarnated souls made themselves known to me in order for their terrible ordeal to be dealt with, and their souls released from the terrible ordeal they'd encountered at the hands of Jack the Ripper.

One of Jack's victims was pregnant when she was murdered, and consequently the baby died, but the soul of the baby took some of the negativity with her in order to deal with the evil vibration that Jack had created during his reign of terror but to deal with it at some other time. Heaven is here on earth but in another dimension, and we need to deal with any negativity in the physical body because that's the vibration that the unjust deed was committed in. So that's why we come back into an earthly life to deal with our negativity because within the realms of heaven negativity or emotions do not exist.

I had a friend who I'd met from time to time, and I always felt that there was something dark about her, she was a lovely person but seemed a bit of a lost soul. She'd often expressed that she wanted to come and see me for a healing session but never did. Then one day years later she arrived with her mother, has her mother needed healing, what transpired was that the mother was the reincarnation of my own mother back in 1888, and we were both overwhelmed by the recognition of the other. Mary was born in Ireland and my reincarnate mother had always had infinity with Ireland and never knew why, she said at times the erg to visit Ireland was overwhelming that at one time she'd considered moving there.

The mother sat down and I gave her healing, she told me that within this life she'd given birth to her daughter, and didn't know she was pregnant with her until she went into labour. As you can imagine it was quite a shock for her, and she'd often asked herself how was it possible that she didn't know she was pregnant?

Her daughter then had her healing session, and much to our surprise she turned out to be the reincarnation of the spirit of the child that had died because of her own mother's demise at the hands of Jack. We discovered that she was carrying within her, the negativity of the reign of Jack, and it had to be dealt with here on the earth plane. She had been re-born into this century for this mass-negativity to be dealt with at the same time as all the other victims that had also come into my life to do. I also dealt with Jacks negativity as well!

I believe the mother had not known she was pregnant with her daughter because it was important that no harm or influence affected the child whilst in the womb because of what she was carrying within her. The mass-negativity was dealt with at the time of her healing session, and straight away her energy changed as the darkness within and around her disappeared, as the mass negativity was eradicated. We don't realise how we are all interconnected, and re-born into the same families or soul group, with us going from lifetime to lifetime together in order to help each other overcome their life's purpose.

The mission of all souls is to eradicate the world's mass-negativity because Jesus Christ did exactly that on his crucifixion. There our souls within the world today who are dealing with, and eradicating the mass negativity that Jesus took with him in order to ease peoples suffering. They say that the spirit of Jesus walks the earth plane today but it's not part of my mission or journey but others to help sort the mass-negativity out. I have a dear friend who went on a pilgrim two years ago to do just that. We all play are parts in ridding our world of negativity that's been accumulated over centuries in order to create a better world and future for us all.

The process of the purification and cleansing of the world structure and humankind will have us all eventually playing our parts. We must all achieve peace within us in order to let go of the unrest of our souls, enabling us to create balance and harmony between all things, and achieve our own inner peace that would eventually allow us to achieve world peace.

We are all fighting our own inner war, because we all have, and still are paying the price of our miss-deeds over the many incarnate lives that we've had since time began. We have all been quite oblivious over the centuries of what we've been doing to ourselves and our world, buts it's only now that we have to make real progress in creating a better world for us all.

The Age of Aquarius gives us all the opportunity to eradicate human suffering, and we must all take an active part in achieving this. So whether it's just individual negative imbalances that we're dealing with or past lifetimes that effects us at time to time or whether it's the collective negativity of humankind we must all participate. We have to take responsibility for us and our actions, and do our best to achieve our soul's mission by ridding our world of its burden of mass-negativity. We will then create a bright future for us all, once we've reconnected with our higher conscious and ascended self by joining forces with the collective vibration of humankind.

CHAPTER 14

THE GOLDEN AGE OF AQUARIUS

The Golden Age of Aquarius will have us all walking the earth plane has a higher conscious being, having ascended from our lower consciousness, and with us now living the life that was intended a long time ago! Our intended life is a life full of promise and excitement, where we explore the unknown and go beyond our limitations. We simply do this by being our higher consciousness which is a perpetual state of spiritual awareness of our authentic self, and a conscious state that takes us beyond the trappings of the material world. We will all leave this world eventually, in order to start a new life in another evolved dimension.

We are now living in The Golden Age of Aquarius, and the world did not end on 21st December 2012 but carried on regardless of the publicity and ancient prophecies. We all need to embrace the prospects of great possibilities, and opportunities has we allow positive growth and change within our lives. So what does it all mean?

We have all been going through a transformational period with our vibration shifting to a higher level of consciousness. We need to become our truth once more by recognising the truth in all that we do. The Age of Aquarius allows us to go through a cleansing and purification process of the sub-conscious and conscious mind. Which then releases the memories of long ago, with the information of our past lives and truth about whom we really are, and to what our life's purpose as been all about. We all evolve on different levels of consciousness achieving the freedom to choose what rightful action will allow us to fulfil our obligation to our higher conscious or ascended self achieving our limitless potential in all that we do. This will allows us to have clear vision, focus, and clarity in the pursuit of our truth about all aspects of our lives and all lives!

The reconnection to our ultimate truth of all things is the pathway to freedom that would allow us to live our lives in perfect harmony, and all aspects of living our dreams successfully with them coming into fruition. So we must all follow our hearts in achieving our dreams and desires, knowing the memories of all lifetimes are stored deep within our souls, and it's the collective consciousness of us.

At this present time we are all questioning what is to happen in the near and distant future. I have children and grandchildren; and I find the prospects for them very daunting. The only sure thing that we can change is our perception and attitude, of how we are going to deal with the current state of affairs. They say that everything happens for a reason, so what is it all about?

It has been prophesied that our world is going to experience some dramatic changes. With the earth's magnetic field weakening, along with the prediction of the reversal of the north and south poles, is cause for concern. This has already resulted in dramatic climate change and the natural disasters that are happening such as earthquakes, volcanoes erupting and worldwide flooding, this leaves us with devastation and disruption to our lives. These disasters are already happening with flooding becoming a big problem, has our climates are changing dramatically.

Over the next few years or so, we will see a lot of natural catastrophic changes to our planet, with us all having to adjust. The Age of Aquarius is about the cleansing and purification of our planet, also with a spiritual transition period of the purification and cleansing of humankind. We are all being made aware of the natural changes that we all need to make, in order to continue our life on earth with us achieving a prosperous life.

At present we are all struggling with the different aspect of our lives, not being sure of what to do? The majority of us struggling on a day to day basis, with the fears of how are we going to cope? Putting our heads down, is not always the best solution of thinking that this time will pass? We seem to go from crisis to crisis, but why? Are we really out of control or is time running out? To be accepting of what in-fact is going on within our lives, will make it easier for us to adjust. To alter our perception to the different situations or circumstances that we find ourselves in; will release us from the controls that we hold ourselves too.

We must have courage and take back the control of our pre-agreed destiny, reconnecting us to our truth, so whatever happens to us we must be accepting because we would have pre-known. In acceptance of what happens to us would have saved us from pain and grief knowing that we can overcome and cope with any situation we find us in. This is the pathway we chose and it's all part of the divine plan, and our continued spiritual growth of our soul just to see if we have learnt our lessons successfully.

So what does the future hold for us? The Age of Aquarius is upon us; it demands codes of conduct from us all, and with each evolutionary age, come the different trends and cycles. With the Age of Aquarius come a lot of changes, some of which will not be pleasant, but whatever happens we should be prepared for. This new Age encourages us to be aware of spirituality, holistic and alternative medicines, the different cultures and our higher consciousness. It's about reinventing and rediscovering our authentic selves once more, and to know the truth about the different events that will happen to us, within this lifetime.

The new age of spirituality is about each person empowering him or her, not just to become successful, but to fulfil their deepest dreams and desires. We do this by being able to survive and overcome our difficult times, transforming ourselves and our lives. This will allows us to achieve our limitless potential by activating our instinctive survival abilities. There are a lot of spiritual traditions and practices readily available, how we choose which path to follow is up to each individual, and to their interests. Spiritual pathways all have one purpose, for they are not just a way of life they are the different methods of achieving a life consciously, and in doing so, enables us to find our inner-selves through the process of spirituality. We do not find ourselves within the different cultures and techniques, but through them, allowing ourselves the opportunity for spiritual and personal growth.

The twenty-first century has new beginnings for us all; we must find our personal resources to meet the challenges in order to transform ourselves. We must have the courage to set off on the soul's journey, to enable the reconnection with our ultimate power of our truth. The future is about accomplishing our dreams and to be living our lives, effortlessly. To achieve our personal inner peace, allows the vibrations within to radiate outwards into the world, eradicating human suffering and enabling World Peace.

The simple pleasures of life create a Well Being state, it also give us quality time with nature, pursuing our interests and talents. When we allow creativity into our daily lives, we are able to express our truth in all that we say and do. In achieving the reconnection of the higher self and that of our higher consciousness, will allow us to live with balance and harmony, maintaining a healthy mind, body and soul. We can then elevate the stress and tension, granting us with more energy and vitality whilst pursuing our dreams or goals. With determination, strength and the right attitude, we can accomplish anything that we want too. We just need to have faith, belief and trust in us and to what we're doing, and that the future holds great things for us all.

During the Aquarian age we will experience some very hard times, with some of us having our lives thrown into chaos. But the most important fact is about the changes to each individual. We will experience changes to our physical body's energy field, the corresponding effects of the earth's and solar systems energy, all changing due to the magnetic field weakening and reversal of the poles. There are scientists, as well as ancient calendars and tribal prophecies, predicting the end of the world, as we know it. Not necessarily the end of the world full stop, but with catastrophic proportions of our world changing. Within each and every-one of us is a Chakra system, meridians lines and acupuncture points. Within the earth's structure is a Chakra system, meridian lines and acupuncture points, all of these will dramatically change with the weakening of the magnetic field.

We must all embrace spirituality has it's becoming a way of life, in order for us to survive these changes; we must prepare the mind, body and soul and re-educate us. We need to bring our vibrations to a higher conscious level, in order to evolve with these changes and times, allowing ourselves the opportunity of not being left behind. We must be able to participate in the spiritual transformation of our world, and we will all experience great phenomenon. The opportunities arise to allow us with the clearing of the subconscious or conscious mind of our repressed and negative emotions. This allows the uplifting of consciousness, with us all becoming a part of the collective consciousness of humankind, once more.

Our past lifetimes are about us bringing our consciousness into the future, to project and manifest all that we desire, and in doing so, we can improve the outlook not just for us, but for others too. We need to actively counterbalance the negativity, help heal human suffering and re-educate ourselves to be less demanding on our resources. We need to be part of the collective consciousness to rid our world of its mass-negativity. We all have to play our conscious part, firstly achieving it for ourselves, then others and then our planet. We are re-cycled souls, time travellers, aiming to undo all that we've done or perceived wrongly in the past, which has added to our present climate, and with the slow decline of our planet and ourselves.

We have brought this on by our constant needs and wants, adding to the demands made upon our natural resources. Maybe our planet is meant to have the natural disasters, to slowly claim back its original origin, an evolutionary cycle. With extinction being a natural part of the earth's journey to naturally rest, to regenerate, and restore balance and harmony which really is no difference to that of our soul.

You would think that we would have understood the consequences of our actions by now. But if everything does happen for a reason then maybe the theory is! With the earth only being a small part of creation, just as we are only a small part of the real us, are we all moving onto other dimensional levels, realms or even other planets in the future because the earth as reached its cyclic end? Or are we going through purification and cleansing process to carry on living on our planet or is the process in readiness of completion of our time on earth as we know it, but this theory could still be centuries away?

The reconnection to the life force energy and source makes us whole once more, giving us a more collective awareness of what it's all about. The Age of Aquarius aids the reconnection of that source and our higher consciousness, enabling us to achieve our goals and ambitions at a much higher level of existence. When this happens, we accomplish our potential by becoming a limitless being once more, allowing us to pursue the experiences and adventures of life, to the highest good of all. We must achieve balance within all aspects of our planet, and protect the resources within its structure. When we become our higher conscious self we can draw on the universal energy that sustains all of life and creation, which will serve us all individually and collectively, creating a better future for all.

It was Gods intention that we should live in peace and harmony, but first, we have agreed to sort the imbalances out, whether they are personally, to others or to our planet. In achieving our life's purpose, we will accelerate our journey into the twenty-first century, where we can make great changes that will affect the whole of creation. We have no control over the governments and the decisions they make, but even if we object and express our views they will not change anything in the short term, as everything takes time to instigate.

The things that we can change, is how we individually perceive the difficult situations, and to the way we allow them to affect us. We do not have to buy into the negativity that comes with the repercussions of their actions. But we can and should address the negativity and to how it affects each individual in order to eradicate it, so we can accomplish our goals successfully.

The future holds a lot of uncertainty, but if we allow ourselves the opportunity to reconnect with the truth of the higher consciousness, we would then become much more understanding and accepting of what's actually going on. So what is going on? A nation fighting for control, there are no winners, just innocent people losing a battle that they have no control over. All of us becoming the victims to the cause and effect of all actions, but if all of life has a purpose, what is that purpose? We have experienced many lifetimes fighting for causes that we believed to be right. With the theory that everyone is right in what they do, then no-one is wrong in what they believe or pursue.

We all fight for what we believe in, but these beliefs change with every lifetime that we have, in order for us to experience all aspects of life. There are no losers, if we can learn from what life is all about. It's not about fighting political wars, but to conquer the war within the unrest of the soul. A product of our miss-guided beliefs of fighting for things outside of ourselves that we really do not have any control over. Fighting for a cause where the real truth of what it's all been about, is kept from us, often with innocent people getting hurt.

Over the centuries, the unrest of the nation as manifested in world suffering with the veils of deceit keeping us all in the dark. Political battles will always continue because of the controls, our personal battles do not have too. We have freedom; we just didn't realise the control that we have over ourselves. To be free, is to give up the things that we have no control over and to be accepting of all things, then we're able to reconnect to the truth that would set us free from the restraints and restrictions within our lives.

The future only holds uncertainty because we have strayed from the source within. When we are at one with ourselves, would allow us to become All Knowing, by sensing our truth and purpose in life. We need to understand that when we have reconnected and become the power of our truth, would allow us to be more trusting and accepting of what happens to us. Knowing that whatever happens was meant to happen, all being a big part of the divine plan. We must believe that we will become stronger and wiser, and that we would be able to cope with any eventuality.

We have to believe in ourselves totally, to understand our potential and unique abilities, it's important to have a clear vision of what we want to accomplish, and to the reasons why we want to accomplish them. The future holds great things for us all, but first, we must allow ourselves the opportunity to be open to our life's lessons, and to receive the information that's needed in order to learn from them. To know our truth in all situations, would allow us to be more accepting of all that's happened, good or bad. This process allows the positives aspects of those learning's to carry us forwards, through the different challenges that we must experience, as part of our life's path.

We must be able to forgive, and to surrender all the things that have not been beneficial to our Well Being. We must also surrender to our thoughts because when we are no longer attached to our thoughts or emotional issues, we'll able to find the solutions to our problems much easier. If we could just image ourselves to be empty of any thoughts, beliefs, preconceived ideas, old programming or fears, we would then be in a position in which to receive the answers to the questions that evade us. When we have achieved a positive mindset, it will allow the mind, body and soul to be influenced by the higher vibration of our higher consciousness, allowing us to be all knowing, but naturally.

In enlightenment, we would become all forgiving, all accepting, all trusting and to have the faith to know that everyone is living out the different aspects of their own truth. So we can all overcome the many obstacles within our lives, helping us to achieve a Well-Being state. When we surrender our worries and issues to God, would allow them to be sorted at a higher level of consciousness. This grants us with freedom to become free of all restraints and restriction with our lives, in order to receive all that we need in attaining a healthy life, evolving to a higher vibration where all that we need to sustain a healthy existence will be revealed.

For future growth, we need to unite with the more refined vibrations of our planet, a transition from the lower consciousness to the higher consciousness. We could then explore the many pathways of spirituality consciously, transforming our lives and allowing us to experience our uniqueness and authentic self once more. This will allow us to achieve our dreams, knowing that we are seeking happier times where we can enjoy our accomplishments.

Our future does not have to be all doom and gloom; we can evolve to the higher vibrations so that the negativity does not affect us anymore. In achieving our higher conscious abilities, allows us to walk the earth plane detached from all negative emotions and suffering. This enables our positive nature to counteract some of the negativity, helping others to achieve their goals and ambitions.

Actions speak louder than words, positive vibrations influence all those that expose themselves to it, leaving them feeling uplifted and energised. This allows them to seek what they need successfully and instinctively, in maintaining a state of Well-Being, that keeps us connected to the source of the universe, and the power of divinity that sustains all growth.

This is the time of new beginnings for us all, not giving into the uncertainty of what our future holds, but to be living in the Now would allow us the opportunity to explore the next evolutionary age with confidence. We will all experience some incredible in-sights into our higher conscious abilities, and of the natural gifts of extraordinary phenomenon. With some of us having out of body experiences, astral travel, remote vision, the third eye opening and our altered state of awareness. This allows us to be more accepting of these unique and instinctive gifts of survival, helping us to maintain balance and harmony with all things.

There is nothing to fear within these gifts, for they are our natural abilities, the higher vibrations allowing them to become activated so that we can achieve great things naturally. We are pure energy being affected by the changing energy of our planet. We are all participating in the purification and cleansing of our planet, and the restoration of balance and harmony.

The Age of Aquarius is the beginning of a new way of life with us all participating in the transformational period that will take us a few years yet, before we really appreciate what's happened to us all. Our new found higher conscious awareness, and with our gifts, skills, talents and abilities, will have us all joyfully experiencing our journey of the soul's quest into ascension whilst still living our life to the full.

With this new age we must all rejoice in what we already have within our lives, focusing on our accomplishments, and to the people that we hold so dear. So everyday in everyway we should be thankful for the pleasures that we all share, reaching out to one another. We can offer support and comfort, encouraging all onwards, but also in making sure that we all have everything that we need to maintain health on every level of existence. This will ensure positive growth on our spiritual pathway, and for the benefit of future generations to come, where we can pass on the infinite knowledge and wisdom.

I believe that the future is not all doom and gloom; I think we are in for a very exciting and rewarding time, once we've overcome the purification and cleansing period. But also to trust that everything within our lives is being overseen by a power, more powerful than anything that we've ever encountered before, with us all going through a process of spiritual initiations.

We are living in a dimensional world, there is a lot more going on than we could ever possibly know or even fully understand in a human form. But if the inevitable happened with the destruction of our planet, we must have belief, faith and trust that we would be ensured a place, in the next dimensional realm. To be all knowing, we would have the belief, faith and trust, to be all accepting, knowing that everything happens for a reason, and the reason is the earth's natural course of evolution.

The future will allow us the opportunity to gain the greater understanding of our purpose, enabling us to recognise and reach our potential. We will have died and be reborn again, maybe many times before our planet earns it's rest, with the distinction of life as we know it. But more importantly, we have all got time to make a difference to the souls continued journey of the completion of our soul, and with the reconnection of the higher conscious self and ascension.

We could live on this planet with very little resources, as long as we were no longer depending on the things outside of ourselves, for survival. Our inner resources could sustain a healthy, happy and contented life, once we had reconnected to them. Not just achieving great wealth but abundance within and throughout our lifetime. This will allow us to use the infinite power of our achievements in other future incarnate forms.

The overall journey in the completion of the soul enables us to become All Knowing and the collective consciousness would allow us to be All Encompassing with everything and everyone, with us all eventually returning to the source of Divinity. This allows us to become whole and complete once more, waiting for the cycle of evolution to start all over again.

We are like the Phoenix as it rises from the ashes of the old self, every 2,000 years. The Age of Aquarius is the rising of the new us has we embrace this golden age from the ashes of the old us, and our world. Evolution is about re-educating us to become our genius self, with the reactivation of our spiritual gifts, making us all unique individuals with us striving for better times and future.

The spiritual awakening of our world, will have us all using more of our brain capacity and hearts energy, and with the awakening of our pineal gland comes the upgrade of our DNA. We will be all using parts of our brains that have been dormant for thousands of years; spiritual awakening will allow us to activate our Astral Bodies, and to be at one with the greater us. With us all eventually walking the earth plane in an ascended existence, with us naturally eradicating negativity and counteracting all just deeds.

We have a positive future that awaits us, and the time is right for us all to embrace that future with confidence, conviction and courage.

CHAPTER 15

SOUL MATES & TWIN FLAMES

Throughout our many incarnate lifetimes we have all experienced a lot of different soul-mate relationships. Our soul-mates are souls that we have shared close relationships with, and have formed special bonds over different incarnate lifetimes. These souls become part of our soul group or family, and incarnate with us from lifetime to lifetime, with us reconnecting and interacting with. The main purpose of soul-mates is to help each other to evolve and learn from our many past mistakes. Sometimes soul-mates are only in our life for a short time in order to share some lesson or just to help us through the difficult times. Hopefully will be lucky enough spend our lives with them by our side in some capacity, whether husband, wife or even that of a special friend or relative.

I have met five soul-mates in this lifetime, and they all played an important part in my spiritual growth, and helping me achieve learning's from other lifetimes as well as this one. I am hoping that they continue to help me through my ascension, has I've been told this is my last life on earth as we know it as long as I continue on my ascension pathway!

My first soul-mate became my earth teacher, teaching me about the incredible in-sights into other dimensions, sharing information that was relevant to my spiritual journey. He showed me how to activate my spiritual gifts so I could achieve my soul's quest by using them in order to help myself and others understand their life's experiences. I shared hours of discussions with him on various aspects of the paranormal, and he also showed me the power of our positive thoughts, telepathy, healing and projecting of my minds energy, and even that of astral travelling. He came into my life when I needed help emotionally and personally, has I'd been really struggling with different aspects within my life. He offered me moral support, and not just when he was me but from afar, has I felt his presence projected to me almost daily. He believed in me and my abilities even when I didn't, and he was a great inspiration to me. I no longer see my earth teacher but we are still infinitely connected on a higher vibrational level, and his soul speaks to mine in my sleep, and at times my waking state as I often see his face projected before my own.

My second soul-mate made himself know to me years later, and although he'd been in my life a very long time I'd never realised the connection between us. Then one day he told me who he was, he knew things about me that even I'd forgotten has he'd witnessed my life's journey unfold. We experienced an incredible spiritually journey, reawakening memories of a life we'd once shared together. When we touched a vibration would passed between us that had us both jumping almost as if we'd had an electric shock. We could drain each other's energy, and I felt giddy when he held me in his arms.

We only spent three months together but it was an incredible learning adventure. We went to art galleries where we stood looking at a picture, and we would project us into the picture to sense the artist mood of when he or she painted their masterpiece. We would also lose ourselves within a piece of music, absorbed in the rhythm listening for the continuous musical note, again sensing the musician's inspiration of when they composed their composition. We also experienced events that had happened in the past going to places of interest just to sense the spirit as they continued to roam the earth plane. This soul-mate is still with me today, and whenever I'm feeling down I'll received a message from him, and his vibration works it's magic in reassuring me all is well.

My third soul-mate came at a time when I was struggling with my health all part of my negative imbalances that I held within. He introduced me to some alternative holistic technique that reinstated the body's natural healing abilities,

106

regenerating and stimulating a well being state. We share an infinite connection, and we've had several past lives together but in various relationship forms. We also went through a process of healing our past lives together, and understanding how the other felt from the various decisions or just deeds that the other did. This gave incredible insight into the meaning of true love and also unconditional love.

My fourth soul-mate came when I was looking for guidance and reassurance that I was on the right path. His positive mindset and personality gave me a much needed boost with him taking me out of my comfort zone. He gave me sound advice and predicted my future, and so far he hasn't been wrong. This soul-mates ascended self projects himself to me quite often as he continues to guide me through my own path of ascension. I no longer see him in the physical form has he lives in America, but his vibration often projects himself to me, and it's always in a supportive role of encouragement and guidance.

My first husband was also a soul-mate but because of what happened between us we wasn't able to maintain the ultimate connection of soul mates. I sense his vibration even now eighteen years after our divorce, and I know that even though we're no longer together, he's like all of my other soul mates and we're still infinitely connected. If we're going to achieve a soul connection throughout any lifetime, it means that both parties has to play their individual part at maintaining that connection, and at times This isn't always possible as one may not be able to maintain the connection because they have other things they've pre-agreed to do for whatever reason.

We all have free will whilst on the earth plane and we don't always make the right choices or so we think! But whatever the case we have to wait until another lifetime to understand what happened to us within this life in order to put it right. Soul-mates will always there for one another whether in the physical body or even after death because their souls are infinitely connected.

TWIN FLAMES

A twin flame connection has to achieve a higher conscious level in order to complete ascension, and at times it can be touch and go has to whether it can be achieved, without time running out! I knew that my twin connection was coming and had waited nearly six years for it to come into fruition. We both had lots of karmic debt to sort out, and past lifetimes to heal and overcome before we could come together.

We also had to prepare ourselves for our soul's quest in preparation for this twin flame connection. Both twins had to achieve and understand the infinite knowledge and wisdom, and gain the unique understanding of life's existence, and truth of all things. They both had to trust in the process because neither really knew what was expected of them because they'd never been through a twin flame journey before within this life, and didn't really know what to expect without feeling apprehensive.

We all travel through the different lifetimes searching for what we feel is missing within our lives. Not realising that what we're searching for is actually our twin flame self that holds the missing elements of us, and together we would feel whole and complete once more. Couples have met over the different centuries hoping that this time around would be the lifetime where they would meet their twin flame in order to reconnect with in order to ascend together. This allows them both to evolve to a higher conscious level of existence, where they go through a series of spiritual initiations to prepare for their final journey together, whilst on the earth plane.

Once twin flames return to the spirit world they ascend to their original origin. Our twin is the other half to us, and during our lifetime the main purpose of their connection is to be with their twin soul in order to experience the ultimate relationship. How many times have we referred to that saying of our other half, but not really understanding the true context of those words?

Over the centuries twin flames and soul-mates connected in order to heal their previous lives that they shared together, as well as this lifetime, they also needed to heal the earths and universal energies, and help with eradicating the collective negativity of humankind. So how do we recognise our twin flame from a soul-mate? The lifetime that you're destined to meet will be a very spiritual life, with karmic debt being paid back in abundance, and you'll have been through various stages of initiation, where you are prepared for the connection of your twin flame, emotionally, physically, mentally and spiritually.

Some twin flames even after this process will meet and collide, and the connection will not made. This happens if one or both are not totally prepared or evolved enough. When we meet our twin flame, we take the risk that we will not connect properly but collide, and both will go their separate ways until another time. If they both continued to evolve after they've gone their separate ways, they might meet again later within their current life, and if not, would have to wait until another lifetime.

Over the centuries, and if we did not meet our twin flame or connect with them, we would meet them once we had returned back to the source, connecting on the astral plane. We then go through a process of overcoming our life's experiences, and agree another lifetime together in order to try again, and achieve the twin flame connection. We would then pre-agree to the different circumstances and the conditions of that lifetime, in-fact everything right down to the finest detail.

When the time is right, we start our new incarnate life all over again, and the process of our pre-agreed life's path starts to unfold. This is commonly known as our souls purpose, and once achieved we can then become our limitless potential by integrating with all the higher aspects of us. We do this by drawing on the positive attributes of us from other past lifetimes where we've been of a higher vibration, we do this in order to try and achieve our ascension within this lifetime.

Once the connection is made between twin flames a healing process takes place, any emotional, mental or physical imbalances are healed. Then they start the process of healing past lifetimes, and gain the understanding of the pre-attempts they'd made in other incarnate lives where they met their twin flame but collided. Perhaps leaving them devastated or possibly it sent them on a road of self destruction, all because of the frustration or anger that they'd felt. I'd had a past life where I did just that, I came so close to achieving ascension with my twin flame, and because I'd given up when I'd nearly achieve the ultimate connection so in the next lifetime that I had I went on a self destruct journey!

When our last life on earth is reached we'll reconnect with our twin flame achieving ascension whilst still on the earth. The earth's vibration now aids us in achieving these twin flame connections, because for first time in centuries the earth's vibration has also gone through a series of initiation in order for us to achieve ascension. All conditions have to be just right with the realignment of the earths, universe and our individual energy all becoming encompassing.

We reunite as twin flames when our mission on earth is complete having achieved a higher vibrational level of ascension, and when we return to the source we would become an ascended master of our origin, where we can help others achieve their ultimate goal of completion of their twin soul connection. We will all at sometime or other have come close to connecting with our twin flame. Maybe with us not realising it because we were not ready! You will be amazed how many times we've been with our twin flame, and then something went wrong and it caused us to go our separate ways!

My twin flame finally made it, and has we looked into each other's eyes we felt the others soul, and the connection was made. We could not draw our eyes away and we were both beaming and blissfully happy as we embraced, not wanting to part. Our chakra's, meridians and acupuncture points all came into realignment with balance and harmony restored to us both, has our bodies swayed whilst still in each other's arms. The recognition was beyond anything I'd ever felt to-date, and was totally different from my soul-mate connections.

We knew each other instantly and the recognition was an incredible experience. We each held within us the missing elements of the other. Even though I was female I was the masculine energy and he was the feminine energy of the twin flame connection. Over the different centuries we have all had the different roles of feminine or masculine genders. The vibration of all souls has to be feminine and masculine energy in equal measures.

With my twin flame now in my life, we realised how our lives were so similar with almost a parallel existence. He only lived a few miles away from where I lived, yet we'd never met until we were ready for the connection. I knew every line on his face; I had seen him so many times in my dream state, and I had been searching for him for the last six years, and I knew I would know him when we met.

The night that I finally met him I'd felt his presence as soon as he walked into the pub, and has I watched him standing at the bar the atmosphere within the room changed, and I found myself back in the Victorian age as I watched a policeman in a Victorian uniform standing by his side, and also a vision of myself in a long blue velvet dress as we stood laughing together. The vision disappeared as he turned and smiled at me, I was distracted for a second and when I glanced over to the bar he was gone. Later I became aware of him as he was suddenly walking towards me, and he introduced himself, his name was Gary.

The connection between us was unbelievable as we had the same likes and dislikes; we were like a drug to the other and we felt we could not be apart. I found that his sleep pattern influenced mine, as we found ourselves awake at the same time even though we didn't live together. We often told the other of when we awoke during the night and much to our amazement it was always at the same time. I could feel his anguish or excitement as he could mine, and I would pick the phone up just before he called or would see his face in my minds eye when he was thinking of me. We taught each other the others abilities, gifts and skills, and we shared our learning's and our understanding of our life's experiences.

When we were together we could perform instant healing and our vibrations went through the roof leaving us in a blissful state. We activated many of our past lifetimes together, some quite disturbing as we dealt with what had happened to us at the hands of others. We had other lifetimes where we were blissfully happy, and our lives were content and very fulfilling.

We healed past trauma and negativity from past lifetimes where the dark forces fought the light! Some of the world's mass negativity was beginning to be eradicated, and dealt with. Like minded souls now came into our lives in order for us to help each other to achieve our own definitive pathways. We all had to help and encourage each other, because no-one person had all the answers, but within each of us was the hidden secrets and truth, about our journey of ascension.

When we were together our psychic gifts would have more clarity and vision, and we would be more knowing because what the one didn't know, the other would. We'd say the same things at the same time, and we'd have the same thoughts or mood swings. Each of us was totally aware of the others feelings or ailments, illness and negative problems that was within our lives, and once discussed they were dealt with instantly.

Twin flames have not met and connected on the earth plane in a long time because the earth's vibration has not been right. The duality of a twin flame connection is in order to help humankind to evolve the limitations of an earthly existence, which helps our planet with positive growth, purification and cleansing. The more attune we become to our planets many needs, the less negative effect we'll have on our resources which creates the many environmental issues. The soul's quest is to set us free from the restraint and restriction that we hold us too, by eventually reconnecting to our higher conscious and ascended self that will allow our twin flame to find us or us them.

Sadly my twin flame connection is no longer within my life, and we went our separate ways. I'm not sure whether we connected properly or collided has only time will tell. We had a past lifetime together in the early eighteen hundreds where he was ready to ascend and I was not, and within this lifetime I was ready to ascend, and he was not because of personal reasons.

The connection we made together has made a difference to me, as I'm sure it has with him, but we no longer communicate. I feel more whole since the connection was made with him, and because we are both aware of the other, I'm sure we'll still achieve what we set out to achieve within this lifetime. Maybe in the future we may meet again in order to continue our quest together?

What I've understood from the experience with my twin flame was that love is infinite and survives the lower and higher conscious realms. We do not have to be physically together to achieve what we set out to achieve, because this is a vibrational world, and we can achieve what we have pre-agreed too, by connecting to the collective consciousness of all that we've ever been since time began, and that includes our original origin.

My ascension journey is ongoing, and even I can't predict the future in order to really know how it all ends or to what evolution really is all about. The more I become my ascended self the more accepting I am of all eventualities, and deep within my sub-conscious is the key to reveal all the mysteries of our kingdom.

CHAPTER 16

THE PATH TO ASCENSION

Our pathway to ascension started a very long time ago, and I believe at sometime or other we were ascended whilst here on the earth plane but many centuries ago. We became detached from our ascended consciousness back in 100,000 BC, and by 8,000 BC we were totally detached. Over the centuries since, we have struggled to maintain our higher consciousness, with us fluctuating between our higher and lower conscious awareness or abilities, which greatly affected our lives. We have all been travelling the journey of our soul's quest in order to reconnect to our higher conscious self once more. Once this is achieved we can start the process of going through the different spiritual initiations in order to maintain a higher conscious existence with us eventually reconnecting to our ascended self. We then continue to experience life as a higher vibration whilst travelling the journey of ascension to enlightenment.

Ascended masters are beings that have lived many lives, and have ascended the realms of conscious living. They were ordinary humans that over the centuries have undergone a series of initiations achieving spiritual transformation. They are the skilful messengers of god, whose main purpose is to serve humanity, helping us to restore faith, belief, and trust in our unique-selves once more. Ascended masters are the protectors of the sacred symbols and geometry, and the infinite knowledge and wisdom that allow us to connect with the collective consciousness of mankind. This enables us to activate the hidden secrets of our natural gifts, skills and abilities, and our limitless potential of all lifetimes. These masters have chosen to come back to earth at this particular time, in order to walk amongst us once more. Helping us all to evolve, and experience The Golden Age of Aquarius consciously, and aid us with the reconnection of the creator's unique power of divinity that resides within us all.

Ascended masters were at one time the figure heads of society, such as kings, queens, heads of state, leaders in battles and crusades, in fact any great person listed as a ruler of their time, and worthy of historian value. These figure heads fought for causes or beliefs that they held to be absolutely true, they had honour, and respect for all things, and were the crusaders of victory. The ascended masters have attained and understood all aspects of the infinite knowledge and wisdom. They have integrity whilst in pursuit of victory, and withhold justice and rightful action, and have incredible powers that aid us all with the completion of each individual's soul's quest.

These masters have experienced all walks of life, and have lived in times of great wealth and prosperity over the centuries. They lived in ancient times of history such as, the time of Jesus Christ, the Egyptians or Atlantis, the Romans and other historical times and places. They have devoted their time to help us ascend the limitations of our lower conscious self, with the reconnection of our higher conscious self, and truth. These masters also aid us on our paths of ascension, where their teachings allow us to reconnect with the God's infinite energy where we'll become enlightened. The refined energy and vibration of these masters will instil us with great potential, purposeful action and intention, allowing us to achieve a higher conscious state in order to achieve our limitless potential.

The ascended masters maintain order to inspire and encourage us in order to attain higher vibrational levels of existence. We can then ascend our limitations of lower conscious living which will enable us to achieve our mission in life, by fighting for freedom from our negative beliefs, programs, and imbalances that are held within our subconscious and conscious minds. To become our higher ascended self once more requires commitment and dedication to the quest of achieving an ascended consciousness, in a

116

human form. There are a lot of people today walking the earth plane whose main objective is to transcend from their higher conscious level into a state of ascended consciousness. So what does this all mean?

Over the years of travelling my own personal, and spiritual journey of self awareness, and an enlightened state as concluded in my conscious awareness of what the process has been all about. We all have the different abilities of psychic awareness, clairvoyance, clairaudience, clairsentience and so on; only they are not really known by those names, they are our natural gifts.

These abilities are our natural senses or gifts like self belief, faith, trust, and self love or a knowing! With us listening to our intuitive senses or gut reactions to what we consider to be our truth or rightful action. It's about seeing our truth, hearing our truth, and speaking our truth at all times, allowing us to feel fulfilled in all aspects of our life. When we listen to our positive thoughts and feelings, allows us to become more knowing. Over a period of time of us using these incredible gifts our knowing will become stronger and stronger, with us eventually becoming All Knowing about all things, but when we need to know, and not when we want to know. This happens because we have reconnected with the collective consciousness of humankind, and the Creators energy which makes us more conscious aware of all aspects of us.

When I started my spiritual journey I prided myself in the fact that I made decisions easily, and acted on my gut reactions, listening to my thoughts or feelings. By not questioning my decisions or choices that I made, I was able to go with the flow of life, knowing I'd made the right decision. Then my life's purpose and lessons started to unfold, I questioned my decisions, and things started to go wrong. I stopped believing in myself, and I started to look to others for recognition or validation that what I was doing was right! Not realising over the years that self doubting was costing me dearly. The more self doubting, the more procrastination that I did, the more the negative imbalances crept into my daily life to the point of making me feel powerless to the decisions that I had to make.

These are the lesson we all learn over the period of our lifetime, but what I understood was that the people I looked too for recognition or validation, I was basically saying that they were more powerful than me! I didn't realise that I was giving my unique power away by doubting myself or even invalidating me by asking others for opinions about my life. At the end of the day no-one knew me better than myself! I knew my positive qualities, and negative short falls, I knew my true self even if I only saw her from time to time. She was the person I was striving to be, the real me, who was radiant, confidant, and compassionate about life, and others. This was the person who was my higher conscious self, and I had to reconnect with her once again she was my higher conscious self.

So my spiritual journey had begun all because I was looking for what I felt was missing within my life. I did not realise until years later, and after experiencing lots of different aspects of the paranormal that what I seeking was my own natural gifts, skills, abilities, and obtaining the truth of all things. I had all of these gifts before I started my journey of understanding what my life's purpose and lessons were all about, but then had stopped believing in them not really knowing there importance. The series of spiritual initiations that I went through was part of my life's journey in understanding the importance of reconnecting with my unique gifts once more, all being part of my higher conscious self that would allow me to seek ascension.

Our life's lessons are a natural process that most of us go through in order to fully understand, and gain a deeper understanding of what is expected from us as our life's experiences start to unfold, and by reconnecting with the positive aspects of us and our unique gifts, we will instinctively know what we can ultimately achieve. Our pride and ego gets us into all sorts of trouble but it's also our survival instinct kicking in which is fed by our own unhappiness. All brought on by our lack of understanding to the bigger picture of our lives. The more we travel away from our truth the harder it seems to reinstate, and our truth is the blueprint of all that we've been, and to what we have accomplished or overcome. Our soul holds the blueprint of the secrets which unlock our gifts, skills and abilities of our higher consciousness, and ascended self in order to reinstate within us, and to use for the highest good of all.

When we've embraced the power within we become self and spiritually aware, we then reinstate self-belief, faith, trust and self-love within us once again. This process reignites the intuitive senses, and allows us to take action whilst trusting in our gut reactions, with us listening and acting upon our positive thoughts or feelings which allow us to become our limitless potential once more. We must also integrate with the collective consciousness of all our incarnate lives, and especially our higher conscious, and ascended lives. We then reconnect to our ascended self which is the ultimate connection of divinity, and is our authentic self in order to embrace the unique power within.

Our power within can aid us in achieving the life that was intended for us, a very long time ago. So remember, no self-invalidation, procrastination, self-doubting or second guessing you, and then you no longer give your power away by asking others for confirmation of what you already know or seeking recognition for what you do. The justification of our actions or lack of commitment to us dilutes our power within. We cannot argue with the truth, and the truth as no justification, because the truth is the truth!

We need to empower us with self-love, acceptance and recognition, no more thinking about what to do, but action, as actions speak louder than words, and there is strength in silence, and courage in conviction, whilst holding our visions or goals until they come into fruition. We must see our truth, speak our truth, and hear our truth at all times, knowing that we are being our truth. We must be humble, grateful, and have compassion and understanding, and to be kind and considerate of our-self and others, by not judging ourselves or others but most of all, only see the good in all things. This is our unique power of divinity and all of creation.

How do we become ascended? We are all travelling a spiritual pathway with us trying to understand what our lives are all about, and what is expected from us. This journey into the unknown as is our life's purpose, and once we have achieved what we've pre-agreed, we will then gain great insight into the life that was intended for us. When we have achieved this goal we would have an understanding of how we can achieve, and maintain the life that was intended. We then go on another journey driven by the soul, becoming a crusader of the soul's quest, with us fighting and searching for the truth of all things in order to recognise our truth.

I have been on a journey of self discovery for a long time, experiencing all aspects of holistic techniques, and there teachings that help to create well being, and improves our health or gives us the understanding as to why certain things happened to us. The next stage was to become self and spiritually aware, this means being body aware so you can understand what you've done to you. We are all a part of the great power of our creator and we're pure at heart, with the illusions of life that leads us away from that purity and power. No one really sets out to make life hard work for themselves or others; it's just the situations that we have created for ourselves over the many centuries and incarnations, which has resulted in our lack of trust, faith and belief, in ourselves?

So whether we have had just one life or one hundred lives, a lot will depend on what has happened to us, to what this life is all about. You can be assured that we have had more positive lives, than we've had negative ones. The reason being is what would be the overall meaning to life, if God intended for us to suffer and to be unhappy? He did not; all of what happens to us is of our own making.

We chose to come back into this lifetime, because we wanted to gain the understanding of what we'd done to us, and then to put it right with us undergoing a series of spiritual transformations. We are all searching for the time when life really was worth living, with us achieving great things. Somewhere deep within our soul is the memories of such times, and it's calling to us to achieve our dreams within this life. So by going within allows us to reconnect to our infinite truth which makes our lives worth-while and worth-living. When we reconnect with the power of the almighty, our life would then become a testament of our accomplishments of all lifetimes, and that's our truth.

We hypothetically travel the Universe and back again, in search of our truth, and to reconnect with the power of our planet and universe, which serves us well within this lifetime, and all future lifetimes. The evolutionary journey into the twenty-first century has begun; it will take us to the next level of existence on this planet. Life and death go hand in hand, evolving to the infinite level of awareness, and the higher consciousness of the soul. It's a comforting thought to think that there is more to life, than the suffering and strife, all man-made; it can be changed, but not overnight.

To explore into the unknown expands our minds energy, but more importantly it allows us to live the life, that was intended. So let's open our hearts, as well as our minds to the universal energy that's sustained life on this planet since time began. We need to embrace all opportunities, for they are the small steps that lead us to the synchronicities and challenges in life that enables us to reach our limitless potential. We then live our lives with the positive vibrations, skills, talents and abilities from all past lifetimes, successfully reinstated into this lifetime where we live a life really worth living, and one where all aspects of our lives becomes all encompassing.

This completes the journey of self discovery of our soul, and the reconnection to our authentic higher consciousness and ascended self once more. All because we've embraced our power of truth! The chart below shows our different levels of spiritual growth and their understanding.

Levels of Spiritual Growth

PHYSICAL: I exist: beliefs, concepts, illness, thoughts, programming, disease, cause and effect.

MENTAL: I think: perception, feelings, actions, interactions, emotions, a knowing, gifts, skills and abilities.

SPIRITUAL: I Feel: I sense, intuition, awareness, gifts, growth, nurture, knowledge and wisdom.

ASTRAL: I Love: I give, receive, acceptance, forgiveness, inspiring, truth, intention and commitment.

ETHERIC: Higher Self/Consciousness: revelation, peace, harmony, tranquility and joy.

CELESTIAL: At one: Reconnected to life force energy of the universe and cosmic energies.

KETHERIC: Divine Knowing: All Being, Enlightened, blissful, higher concepts and unconditional love.

UNIVERSAL: All Knowing: at one with God. We are then able to manifest our dreams, and become a Limitless Being.

COSMIC: Gods Will: Pure consciousness and grace, infinity, integrity, whole and complete once more.

ASCENSION: Completion of the souls quest, re-birth, light seeking light, Enlightenment and pure essence or origin.

EMERSION: Souls journey of evolution, Superior, Divinity and All Encompassing.

CHAPTER 17

ENLIGHTENED

We are all on our personal pathways to enlightenment, and it's a journey that's spanned over many lifetimes with us all getting close to achieving our soul's quest. We do not have to be on a religious path or even a spiritual path in order to attain being enlightened, as it's a natural process of life of being open to the truth of all things. We experience life with us not always being our truth, but as we seek the understanding of any given situation or circumstance that we find ourselves in, we will eventually recognise the different levels of truth as we evolve and learn.

Over the years of being self-aware and gaining the understanding of what had happened to me, I was able to understand that by being totally honest with myself I could expose the truth of what was happening and the reasons as to why? Everything that we do is influenced by our perception of what we think has happened because of our emotional or mental states and that of our life's purpose. We get confused because everything we do is about our truth but our levels of truth evolve with us, as we see, hear and speak our truth with clarity, we can access our true instantly.

The cost of human suffering has been enormous because of our inability to recognise the truth. We have programmed our minds to believe what it witnesses as been true, because of our limiting beliefs and life's experiences. At times out of necessity what we experience we see as our truth because we need it to be true in order to survive on a day to day basis. The human mind is dedicated to seeking truth, and what it seeks is confirmation of what it already believes, because at times we are incapable of recognising the truth because we take things to personally. We only ever view what's happened to us from our point of view which is very limiting because of our limiting beliefs, emotional anguish or insecurities.

A judge resides over court to witness that the truth is recognised and that justice be done, and a jury decides what's true once presented with the facts, and with an unbiased opinion they can pass judgement. In other words they should be detached from the outcome, and allow themselves to concentrate on the evidence given, by being also detached from their own life experiences or how they perceive life or justice. People who have attended the court to watch the proceedings have an opinion based on what they know or have read about the trail, which then clouds the version of the truth. In simplistic terms we should witness our own lives by being detached from what we think we know, and being honest with us to how we perceive our lives, because we are all blinded because of our limiting beliefs. We have been brain washed and programmed for so long, we honestly do not recognise the truth until our state of conscious awareness or understanding alters or the truth is presented to us, after finally understanding our dilemmas.

We never recognise what's happened to us until we allow us to see the truth; others will see our truth differently as we will theirs. Every-ones truth is only recognisable to them, because of their life's experiences and understanding of what's happened to them to date, and to how they were emotionally, physically or mentally at the time. With every understanding of life's experiences our level of truth alters, the essence of our truth and how it can be recognised, expressed or defined denotes how committed we are to being our truth. The discovery of truth can be known instantly and cannot be argued with or justified, because our truth is just that Our Truth!

So how do we recognise truth? It's understanding that the elements of truth changes with our personal understanding and growth, and with an inner honesty or inner knowing we can recognise our truth instantly. Our truth then becomes more knowing with growth and experience, and when we surrender our negative beliefs or programs, we can access our truth, albeit only the level of truth at that time.

When we have a unique understanding of what we do to us, and by not trusting or being detached from our insecurities, we cannot successfully recognise our truth or anyone else's. To have an opinion of others is not about their truth but ours which is then biased, but also it about not feeling threatened or insecure by others and their interpretation of their truth. We all see truth differently, depending on our life's experiences, and our perception of the knowledge and wisdom.

The truth is a knowing that you can't argue with, and anything other than the truth is justifiable. When we become enlightened to our truth everything within our lives just flows, and we attract all that we need with a deep knowing. A seeker of the truth has to surrender their burdens, thoughts, and outcome to the will of God, also to release self-judgements and to be realistic in the goals that they set themselves. If we need something to be true, it's because of personal gain, our insecurities or perception at the time, and we often have a need to prove that it's true in order to prove something to us or others, instead of just accepting our level of truth.

Our truth is our power within, unique to just us and then to be accepting of others truth in order for us to continue to learn and evolve together. Because our level of truth changes with our understanding of life's lessons or experiences, has does others truth. If we are accepting of each other, and to respect others wishes or decisions, then we will not feel threatened in anyway by others, because we're all being our truth even thought its tainted with our learning's.

Enlightenment means to recognise your level of truth at any given moment, and when we recognise that our level of truth alters with our continued growth and understanding. When I first began to read the works of great philosophers, and gained an understanding of their perception of the higher conscious states of awareness, I was able to recognise my level of truth which eventually allowed me to become enlightened to the different aspects of my life.

The different stages of enlightenment was mind blowing, thinking I'd reached the heightened state of awareness only to discover a few days later that I'd only scratched the surface of infinite knowledge, and the infinite wisdom came from the understanding of each process. We all have a responsibility to us to focus on our own enlightened growth because it's different for everyone, and if we try to replicate others interpretation of an enlightened state, we're giving credence to their version of truth and not ours, which leaves us chasing someone else's belief's or understanding.

Our personal level of truth is first-hand and instantly knowing, and anyone else's is second-hand. So I will try to explain how I arrived at my level of truth, and the unique understanding of what's expected from us. My journey of self-discovery was about self-realisation and the importance of self-belief, faith and trust which then gave me self-love. By not giving my power away, and I listened to my intuitive-self, acting on the information I received gave me a knowing or positive thoughts in order to recognise my truth, because my gut reaction allowed me to know what's right or wrong, and even if the timing was not yet. By trusting myself completely I could recognise my truth because if what I was doing was not about my truth I felt the unrest within instantly.

This process allows us to truly know who we are, with us being totally accepting of every aspect of us, and loving ourselves with all our imperfections that makes us all individual and unique. To know yourself completely gives you conviction, courage, and intention to fulfil your dreams or goals, and not to be fazed by any outward pressures. You must hold the vision of what you want to achieve, until you've brought your dreams or goals into fruition.

To be enlightened is to be totally dedicated to living your life in truth, by seeing your truth, speaking your truth and listening to your truth at all times. Our truth is just that our truth, and to be accepting of others version of their truth or even to walk a mile in their shoes, allows us to recognise elements of their truth which makes us more accepting and tolerant of others. We have judged us and other unfairly, when we offer forgiveness allows us to release any grief or guilt we may have, but also to release any negative beliefs or programs that do not serve the highest good of all. To have the courage to know yourself and to be proud of who you are will allow you to recognise your truth at all times which allows you to become enlightened to the truth of all things.

I have listed below the growth process from the higher conscious self to the ascended self that allows us to continue our journey of being enlightened.

Levels of Enlightened Growth:

Self Belief: To believe in yourself completely and to reinstate self-belief within.

Self Faith: To have faith in you totally by being realistic in your goals and commitments.

Self Trust: To trust you to make the right decisions, with conviction and courage.

Self Love: To love you and to honour and respect you, giving yourself permission to seek the best from life.

Intuition: To listen to your knowing thoughts, truth and not to second guess yourself.

Gut Reaction: to know right from wrong and to know when danger maybe lurking.

Knowing Thoughts: To recognise our positive thoughts from our higher/ascended self that requires action.

Compassion: To show compassion to you and others and to be compassionate about life.

Non Judgement: Not to judge you or others unfairly, knowing that we are all right in what we do.

Tolerant and kind: To care for others less fortunate than you, and to encourage and support them.

Acceptance: In acceptance we find the solutions to our problems that save us from pain or grief.

Forgiveness: To forgive ourselves and others, releases us all from blame, knowing we are all right in what we do, and that we can learn and grow together.

Unconditional Love: To love unconditional without a hidden agenda or reward.

Higher consciousness: To recognise our truth and to be our truth and higher conscious self at all times.

All Knowing: Our knowing thoughts, and to know the difference of our lower conscious thoughts.

Ascension: To see our truth, hear our truth and speak our truth, and to live our life with no attachments.

Enlightened is to be enlightened to our truth and life's purpose, and once we've understood and overcome our learning's we can live the life how it was intended.

In ascension we would only see the good in all things, and we would not live in a negative world but a positive one of great fortune and potential, as our vibrations evolve the material world. We would then be enjoying a life with no attachments or any preconceived expectations, because everything we need would naturally come to us. We are all individual with different backgrounds, and past life history that's unfolding in order for us to learn from. Our life's lessons and purpose is revealing our truth, and true identities of who we really are, making us whole and complete once more.

Ascension is completion of the soul's quest which then allows us a rebirth, with us seeking love, light and truth in all things. Our ascension path leads us to the understanding of a deeper truth of our existence, and a journey of progress where we achieve more by doing less. When we surrender to the will of God, his life force energy sustains all growth, and everything we need is within the collective consciousness of humankind, because we've Embraced the Power Within.

FURTHER INFORMATION

Email veronicalavender@btinternet.com

Website: www.veronicalavendersholisticevents.co.uk

www.veronicalavender.com

I have put this book together as a guideline for an aid for Well Being; it is therefore your own personal choice to take part in any of the techniques described as a possible way of increasing self-knowledge and understanding, and the releasing of negative blocks or disharmonious situations within the energy system by using this balancing technique. I therefore taken no responsibility and no legal actions can be taken against me.

Made in the USA
Columbia, SC
20 May 2017